W9-BWB-704

Composite Materials
Fabrication Handbook #1

John Wanberg

Published by:
Wolfgang Publications Inc.
Stillwater, MN 55082
www.wolfpub.com

Legals

First published in 2009 by Wolfgang Publications Inc.,
PO Box 223, Stillwater MN 55082

© Timothy Remus, 2009

All rights reserved. With the exception of quoting brief passages for
the purposes of review no part of this publication may be reproduced
without prior written permission from the publisher.

The information in this book is true and complete to the best of our
knowledge. All recommendations are made without any guarantee on
the part of the author or publisher, who also disclaim any liability
incurred in connection with the use of this data or specific details.

We recognize that some words, model names and designations, for
example, mentioned herein are the property of the trademark holder.
We use them for identification purposes only. This is not an official
publication.

ISBN number: 1-929133-76-6
Printed and bound in China.

ACC LIBRARY SERVICES AUSTIN, TX

Composites Materials: Fabrications Handbook #1

Acknowledgements

My sincere, heartfelt appreciation goes out to several people who have been instrumental in making this book possible. They include the following:

Metropolitan State College of Denver for providing funding for materials and access to lab space and personnel…

Plasticare, Inc. of Denver, Colorado (www.plasticareinc.com) for product and technical assistance…

My wife, Charlotte, who has unexpectedly become an "expert" in composites herself by assisting in so many long photography, editing, layup, and demolding sessions…

The students of Metro State's Industrial Design department who find composites an interesting enough topic to encourage me to teach and share it with them…

Timothy Remus, for giving me the opportunity to share this exciting topic with other fabricators, do-it-yourselfers, and the innumerable creative souls out there.

John Wanberg

Introduction

Having worked with composites for over a decade now, I'm still surprised that there are so few hands-on books about composites. People frequently ask me if I know of a good reference to help them get started, but I'm always at a loss on where to point them. When I first began to dabble in composites myself, I found that most books rarely discuss the actual "how-to" of composites manufacture. Those books that did deal with composites, covered the subject in a very technical and mathematical manner. Even now, the overwhelming majority of the information available about composites is found in technical journals and manufacturer literature, engineering papers, and college-level manufacturing and engineering textbooks. To be fair, this is due in part to the fact that designing structures that truly optimize the performance of these novel materials requires some respectable skill in engineering and materials science. For many home-built composites applications, though, such a command of engineering physics and chemistry is not really required to make satisfactory components—akin to the realization of how very few metal fabricators actually sit down and determine the load-bearing capabilities and failure modes of their parts though they can still build perfectly sound parts using some general metalworking skills.

At their most basic level, the methods for manufacturing composites are simple enough for most do-it-yourselfers to grasp—and even master—in their own garage or shop space. In fact, most of what I have learned (in the pragmatic sense) about composites has come from getting down and dirty in the shop, mixing up resins, cutting reinforcement fabrics, trying out one lamination method after another, and working the cured composite to a good finish. It is this hands-on approach that, I believe, truly improves one's skills in the fine art of competent composites creation.

Composites, by their nature, are a very hands-on material—something most fabricators quickly realize once they are up to their elbows in sticky resin and furry fibers. Due to the lack of literature on composites fabrication techniques, however, I have observed many people dabble in composites, only to become frustrated by a lack of experience and then despondently walk away from their projects. What I have attempted to do with this book is illustrate the step-by-step simplicity of several composites building processes to help minimize common aggravations. Many of these processes may or may not be relevant to everyone's particular needs, but are presented in this book as a kind of reference "toolbox" from which composites builders can problem solve and confidently tackle their next project.

This book refrains from bogging the reader down in too much jargon or engineering mathematics—although some special terminology is included, as necessary, to convey various composites concepts. The majority of this book covers the subject of composites from a practical perspective, explaining the basic material makeup of composites, formation of composite parts and structures (including multiple molding techniques), mold construction, and even several methods for finishing composite parts for increased aesthetic appeal. As much as possible, this book emphasizes hands-on application to help individuals gain confidence in building their composites projects.

This book has been developed for both students and home-builders alike. Each chapter begins with an introduction to the topics covered, and ends with chapter conclusions for quick access to textual information. Numerous illustrations and photographs aid in visually explaining concepts alluded to in the text. Special terminology is explained within the body of the text, but is also included in a glossary at the back of the book. Moreover, references to additional readings for each chapter are provided at the end of the book to provide supplementary resources for those seeking more in-depth information on the topics discussed.

Unfortunately, in the interest of creating a simplified handbook for the average fabricator, this text will not cover some important aspects of composites common to industry or more advanced composites fabrication. These omitted topics include in-depth composites chemistry and materials science, thermoplastic composites, natural-fiber composites, ceramic or metal matrix composites, vacuum-bagging and resin transfer techniques, compression molding, sandwich structures, automated fiber placement or continuous fiber molding techniques (filament winding, pultrusion, etc.), high-volume composites production techniques, composite structural design and analysis, and composite part testing. In spite of these omissions, I believe it is still important for fabricators to supplement their understanding of composites with additional technical literature that cover such topics. Therefore, as a means to gain a broader understanding of composites, I would encourage readers to seek out other additional texts and resources as required to meet their particular composites needs. The greater your awareness and practical experience in composites, the more you will truly become equipped to fabricate composites—in your shop, garage, or wherever it may be.

Chapter One

Composites Basics

Anatomy of a Composite

"Composites" are materials composed of two or more dissimilar materials. Modern advanced composites consist of fiber reinforcements in a solidified resin. These two materials are joined together through a layup procedure, often to create a laminate. The resulting material has special properties that differentiate it from traditional materials, making it uniquely suited for some applications.

WHAT IS A "COMPOSITE"?

By its most basic definition, a "composite" is any material made up of two or more dissimilar materials. With such a broad definition, concrete, asphalt, particle board, or even paper-maché could be considered composite materials. However, when used in modern engineering, the term composite (sometimes called an "advanced composite") generally refers to a class of

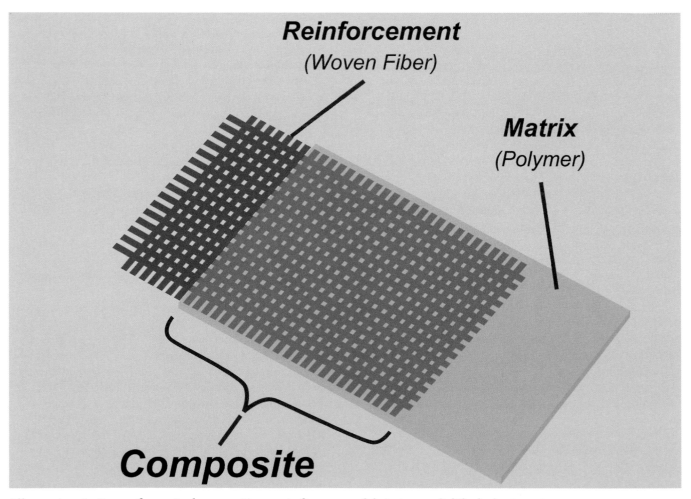

Illustration 1: Parts of a typical composite: a reinforcement fabric in a solidified plastic resin.

materials made up of reinforcement fibers embedded in a solidified material. In such composites, the properties of the fiber and solid material combined exceed those of either of these materials individually. Although several types of advanced composites exist, this text will only explore synthetic fiber reinforcements contained in a solidified plastic or polymer — also known as polymeric composites. (see illustration 1)

MATRICES

The component of the composite that surrounds and holds the fibers in place is referred to as the "matrix" (the plural form of which is "matrices"). The composite's matrix provides the composite's compressive (pressure) strength along with additional shear strength to keep the fibers from shifting in relation to each other. The matrices used in advanced composites can range all the way from polymers to actual metals or ceramics, depending on the performance needs of the application. (see photo 2.)

REINFORCEMENTS

The reinforcement in a composite provides tensile (pulling) strength and some shear (tearing) strength as well. Raw reinforcements have the appearance of simple fabrics — which they actually are — with visible threads and a textile-like flexibility that allows them to be draped over a form. They are supplied in rolls of standard widths, similar to average textiles, and can come in several different woven and non-woven styles. (See photo 3.)

LAYUPS

To form a composite, the reinforcement and matrix are joined together in a procedure called a "layup" or "lamination". During a layup, the reinforcement is infiltrated — or "impregnated" — with resin by rolling, spraying, pressing, squeezing, injecting, or applying a vacuum to infuse it into the fibers. The methods for creating a composite are divided into two major layup categories: wet layup and dry layup. At a basic level, wet layup processes include those methods that require the composites fabricator to actually touch the liquid resin — usually in an open mold — whereas in a dry layup, the fabricator only touches

Photo 2: A common matrix: un-cured liquid epoxy resin.

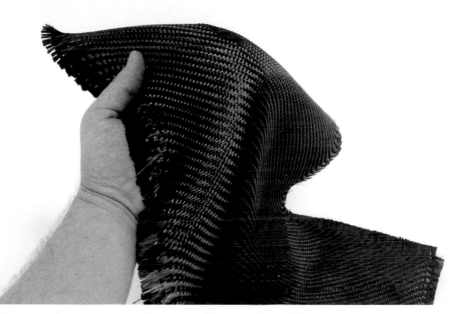

Photo 3: A common reinforcement fabric: carbon fiber.

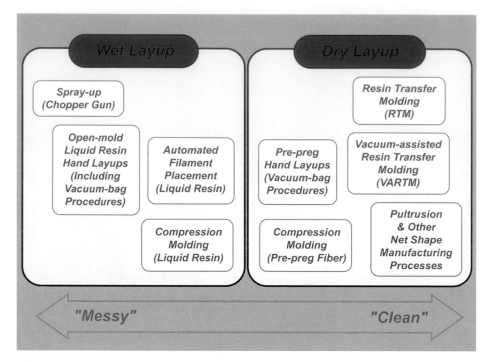

Illustration 4: A comparison of the "messiness" of different wet and dry layup processes.

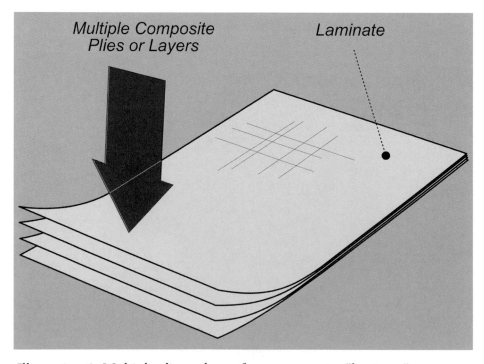

Illustration 5: Multiple plies or layers form a composite "laminate".

the dry reinforcement without directly handling the liquid matrix. Dry layup procedures generally require considerable equipment investment and skill to be effective. (See illustration, 4.)

LAMINATES

Although very lightweight, a single layer — or ply — of composite is usually too flexible for most practical applications. Because of this, multiple plies of resin-impregnated fabric are typically formed together in a mold to create a "laminate". Each of these plies bonds to the next one as the resin cures, creating a unified composite structure. As with other materials, the thicker the laminate, the less flexible it becomes. (See illustration 5.)

One benefit of laminating composite layers together is that the orientation of the fibers can be arranged to control the directional strength of the composite. This is similar to how a single sheet of wood veneer is bendable when flexed across its grain, yet stiff when flexed over the grain's length (see illustration 6). When laminated in alternating directions with other plies of veneer, however, it becomes stiff plywood. Likewise, when a composite's fibers are oriented in one direction, the composite has significant strength over the fibers' length, yet it will flex and bend (or even fracture) very easily when stressed perpendicular to the fibers. For this reason, fabricators will often place the fibers at different angles in the laminate plies to control the directional strength as needed for the design, or otherwise use reinforcements that are woven in multiple directions. When creating plans to show how a layup should proceed, the designer often describes the fiber's directional orientation for each layer in angular degrees measured from a particular reference direction. (See illustration 7).

In spite of the strength added by lamination, composites are not impervious to damage. If a composite laminate experiences too much physical stress —whether through overload, bending, or impact — the fibers, resin, and laminated plies will fracture or separate, creating a condition called "delamination" (or "delam", for short). When composites fracture and delaminate, the results are very similar to broken plywood, where stiff fibers and shards of material are left protruding haphazardly out of the remaining laminate (see photo 8). In less destructive scenarios, where the matrix separates but the fibers do not fracture, delamination may appear as a hazy, lightened area in translucent laminates (like fiberglass) or as a soft or unusually flexible spot in opaque laminates (such as with aramid or carbon fiber composites). (See photo 9).

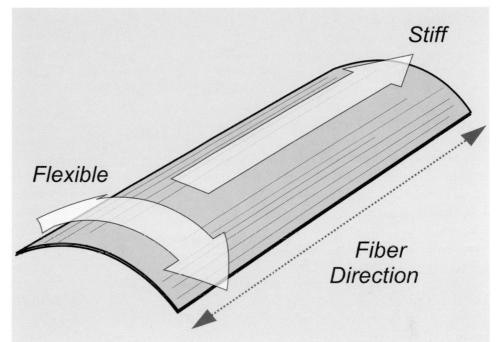

Illustration 6: *A composite is stiffest in the direction of the fibers, and most flexible (or fragile) perpendicular to the fibers.*

WHY COMPOSITES?

Given the broad variety of materials available to industry (and in our case, those available in a small shop setting) it may seem odd that there could be a need for yet another material with which to build projects. Woods, metals, plastics and other materials all have benefits to their use that have been time-tested and are widely understood — so why push them aside for something else? For starters, composites offer certain physical properties that give them an edge over traditional materials. Some of these include: a high degree of strength for their weight, relatively easy moldability (when compared to casting metals or molding plastics), impact and dent resistance, collision energy absorption, weather resistance, tunable directional strength, and

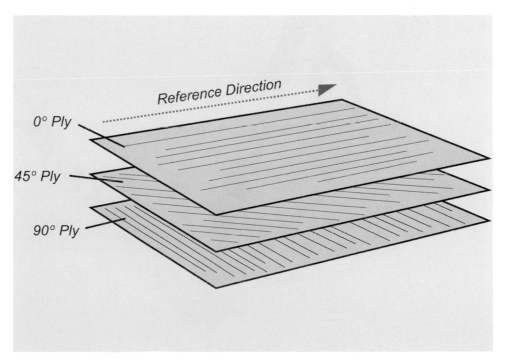

Illustration 7: *Plies with different fiber orientations are commonly described in terms of the fibers' angle in relation to a reference direction.*

even some unique aesthetic qualities.

With such a broad range of beneficial characteristics, it may seem as though composites would be the optimum choice for practically any application — but this is not necessarily the case. Due to their relatively high cost, composites are typically used judiciously when their properties exceed those of other materials. For example, weight savings can be significant when composites are used instead of conventional metals for large parts. However, when used in smaller components, the meager weight savings may not warrant the inherently higher material and production costs. Likewise, some mass-produced products may benefit from composites' higher performance characteristics, but due to their relatively slow manufacturing methods they may take a back seat to other traditional processes and materials.

One thing that makes composites especially enticing to do-it-yourselfers is that they can be created using relatively low-tech tools. In fact, a well-outfitted wood shop, with some other specialty tools mixed in, will usually suffice for most composite mold-making and part fabrication operations. Even if such resources are not readily available, acquiring the power tools and hand tools necessary to build composites requires only a modest investment.

Another benefit of composites is the fabricator's ability to vary the actual make up of the composite part. Dissimilar composite materials can be laid up in the same mold and can even be selectively reinforced in areas that may need added or localized strength simply by adding more layers. Additionally, it is possible to incorporate other materials as inserts in the composite (such as mounting brackets and metal hardware) to minimize part count and inventory, assembly time, and cost.

Even the molds for composites can be made in a relatively short amount of time, with low labor cost, using inexpensive materials. Unlike one-off parts constructed from traditional materials, once you have cre-

Photo 8: The results of a catastrophic fracture on a carbon fiber bicycle frame's head tube—yet another reason to check your car's bike rack before going through a car wash.

ated a mold for a composite part, it can be used to make dozens, even hundreds or thousands of parts, if used correctly — trumping the time necessary to replicate the same custom metal part one operation at a time. The low cost and simplicity of molding alone make composites very attractive to manufacturers of short production run vehicles in forming large exterior and interior body panels and structures. In fact, some manufacturers of exotic automobiles have found that composites are more cost-effective than stamped metal body parts in production volumes less than 70,000 units per year.

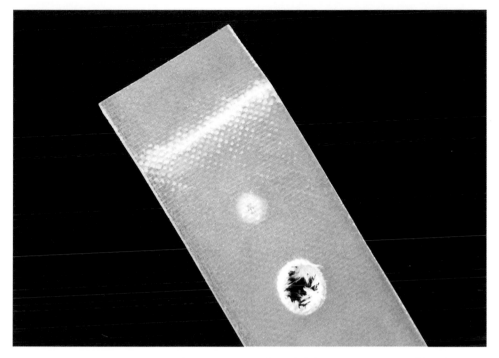

Photo 9: Examples of delamination in a fiberglass composite caused by different stresses: delamination from bending (top), impact delamination (middle), edge delamination caused by a dull drill bit (bottom).

GENERAL COMPOSITE TYPES

In industry, several names are given to composites to help differentiate them from other materials. One acronym commonly used by engineers, designers, and manufacturers to describe composites in general is "FRP" -- or Fiber Reinforced Plastic. Other acronyms describe the fiber component in the composite more specifically, and include the following (see photo 10):

GFRP (Glass Fiber Reinforced Plastic) – This is the most common and inexpensive of the reinforced plastics and is typically called "fiberglass".

CFRP (Carbon Fiber Reinforced Plastic) – This composite is widely used in aerospace and racing due to its excellent stiffness and strength.

AFRP (Aramid Fiber Reinforced Plastic) – These composites have some of the highest relative strength due to the fibers' ability to stretch rather than break.

Without going in-depth into engineering concepts about different aspects of a composite's strength properties (such as yield strength, tensile modulus, etc), the following photographs

Photo 10: Examples of some common composites: fiberglass (GFRP), carbon fiber (CFRP), and aramid (AFRP).

help demonstrate the relative stiffness of various composites compared to traditional materials. The first photo shows samples of steel, aluminum, balsa wood, GFRP, CFRP, and AFRP, all of the same thickness (.030"), width and length (2" by 11") clamped to a solid surface (see photo 11). The stiffness of these samples is already somewhat apparent, even when only supporting their own weight. However, once a weight has been applied to each (in this case, 360g/12.7oz clamped onto the end of each sample) the relative stiffness becomes very clear. Steel and CFRP show the highest stiffness, followed by aluminum and AFRP, then GFRP and balsa (see photo 12).

WHERE ARE COMPOSITES USED?

Although they are not always readily apparent, composites are used in many objects that we may see everyday. As mentioned above, there are specific benefits to using composites that make them especially useful.

Some examples of products that capitalize on composites' unique properties include the following:

Transportation -
Bicycle frames and parts
Exotic sports cars and car parts
Motorcycles
Competition vehicles, Formula 1, CART, NASCAR, Drag, Human Powered Vehicle (HPV), high mileage, etc.
Aircraft and aerospace
Boats
Camper shells
Recreational vehicles and trailers
Semi-truck bodies/trailers
Construction vehicles
Recreation -
Surfboards
Skis and ski poles
Snowboards

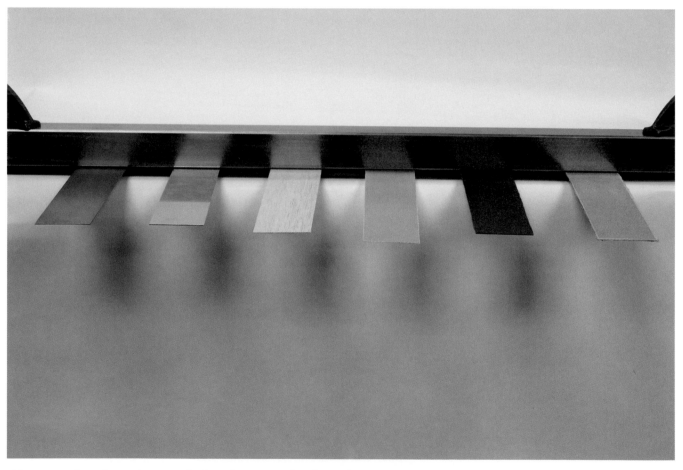

Photo 11: Equal weights attached to these samples show their relative stiffness.

Waterslides
Tennis rackets
Golf clubs
Hockey sticks
Snowmobiles
Jet skis
Industrial/Commercial –
Storage tanks for water, chemicals, and pressurized gas
Circuit boards
Tools such as some hammer handles, etc.
Ladders
Other Miscellaneous -
Artificial limbs and prosthetics
Armored/bullet-proof vests
Corrugated greenhouse roofing panels
Panels on heavy equipment
Microwave transmitter covers
Satellite dishes
Windmill and wind power generator blades
Architectural details, panels, etc.

Statues and sculptures
Outdoor and specialty furniture
Designer jewelry

CHAPTER CONCLUSION

Laying up a matrix and reinforcement into a laminate form, with the reinforcement fibers aligned for directional strength, will result in a composite structure that is optimized to capitalize on the composite's special properties. While composites can be fabricated using relatively inexpensive tools, it is important to consider the cost of the particular materials and the manufacturing processes to be employed. Abbreviations for some different composites include GFRP (Glass Fiber Reinforced Plastic), CFRP (Carbon Fiber Reinforced Plastic), and AFRP (Aramid Fiber Reinforced Plastic), each of which has wide application in many everyday transportation, recreational, industrial, and other products.

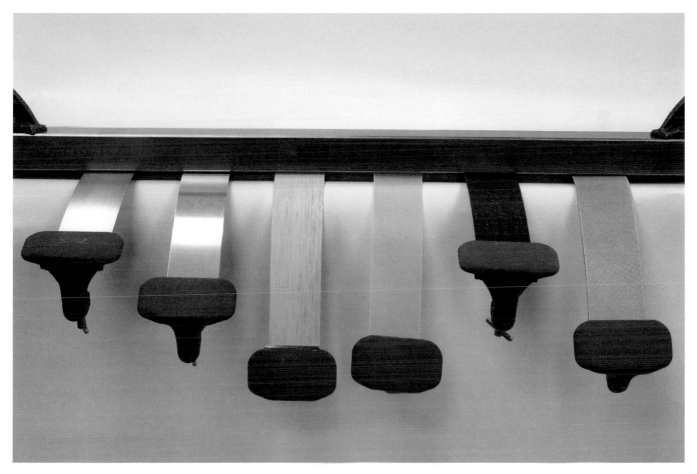

Photo 12: Equal weights attached to these samples show the relative stiffness of the different samples.

Chapter Two

Matrices and Reinforcements

Determining Resin and Fabric Types

Many effective thermoset polymer matrices and fiber reinforcements are available for use in composites. The thermoset matrix solidifies through chemical processes, rigidifying the composite and giving strength to the flexible fabric reinforcements within it. However, to optimize the properties of a composite, fabricators should be conscious of several material aspects prior to layup. While the use and layup of the final composite should be carefully considered, various properties of the matrix and reinforcement have a large impact on the composites performance characteristics.

CHOOSING A MATRIX/REINFORCEMENT SYSTEM

Selecting a resin and fiber combination — or resin/fiber system — for a composite is a very important step in the composites creation process. To do this, the final use of the composite part must be con-

Photo 2: If not used quickly, mixed resin can solidify prematurely in its mixing container, creating a useless paperweight.

sidered from the very beginning to avoid costly material choices or even catastrophic composite failure once the part is put into service. For example, matching a high-strength fiber (such as carbon) to a low-strength matrix (like polyester resin) would not produce the highest level of performance one would desire from a carbon reinforced composite. Likewise, using an abrasion-resistant aramid fiber with a high-cost resin (such as epoxy) for a component without high performance requirements (such as a painted architectural decoration) would be foolishly cost ineffective. The following explanations of resin and fibers along with their various types and properties are provided to help in this important composites decision making process.

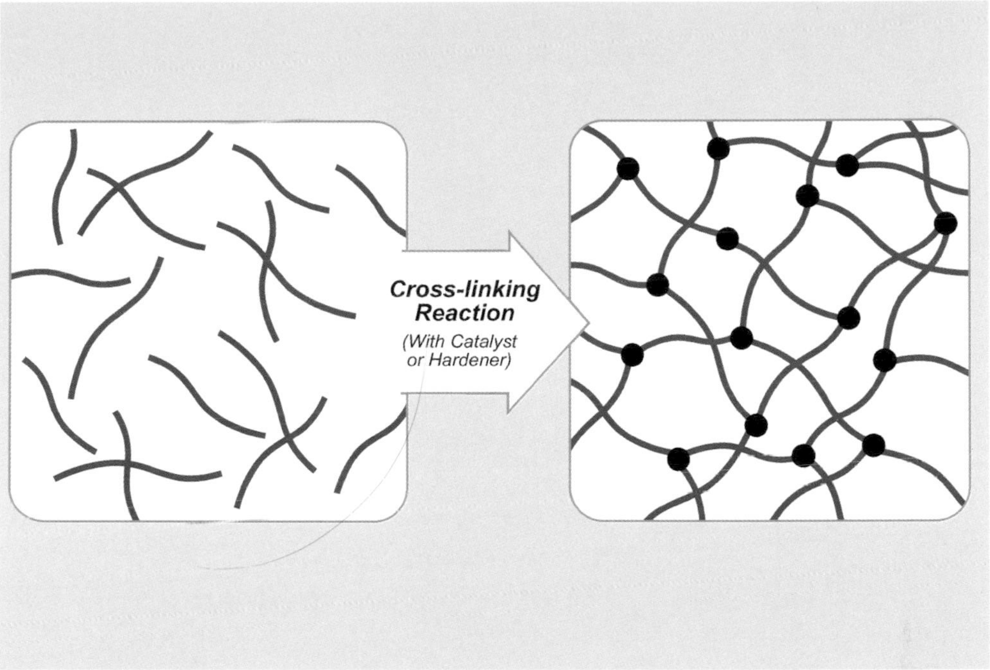

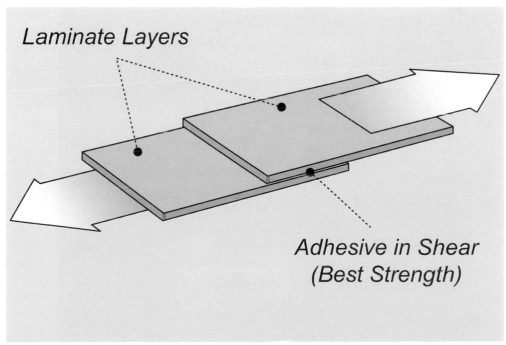

Illustration 1: Resin molecules "cross-link" to join with one another through the addition of a catalyst or hardener.

MATRIX TYPES AND PROPERTIES

While there are various types of polymer matrices available in industry, those resins that are most easily utilized by home builders fall under the category of "thermoset" polymers. Unlike "thermoplastic" polymers that can be heated and melted many times over (like those found in most recyclable consumer goods), thermosets generally start off as a liquid and then — through the addition of a catalyst of hardener — solidify in an irreversible chemical process, rendering them unable to melt at high temperatures. This chemical reaction, called "cross-linking", joins the ends of each polymer molecule with others around them to create a single interconnected and

Illustration 3: Laminates are strongest when forces are applied to them parallel to the plies (in "shear").

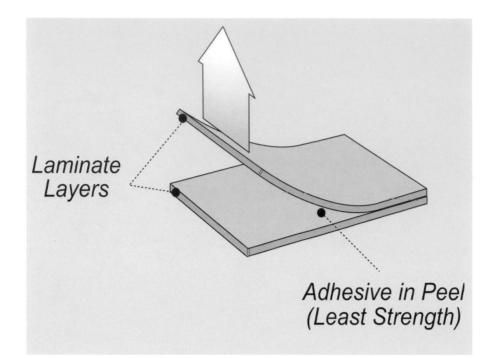

Illustration 4: A laminate is weakest to forces that attempt to "peel" the plies apart.

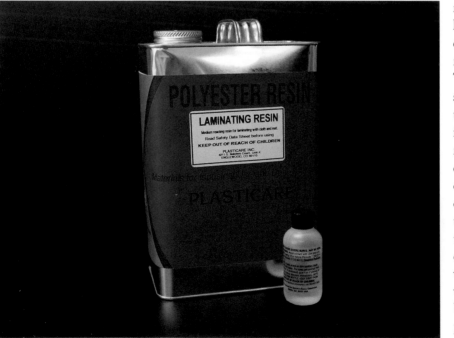

Photo 5: Polyester resin – Inexpensive and easy to use.

very strong molecule (see illustration 1). Common thermoset polymer matrices include polyester resin, vinylester resin, epoxy resin, and other more exotic polymers such as phenolic and polyamide.

One side effect of the cross-linking process is the release of heat energy through an "exothermic" chemical reaction. When the resin is reacting, or "curing", this heat discharge may or may not be very obvious, and is somewhat dependent on the rated cure time for the resin system (i.e., fast cure resins tend to generate noticeably higher amounts of heat). Usually, if a resin is spread into a thin pool, the heat generated by the reaction is very minimal. However, if that same resin is contained in a cup or bucket, the heat generated by the resin within the concentrated space dramatically increases the speed of the reaction, often resulting in a runaway, premature cure (see photo 2). This self-feeding reaction may even generate enough heat to soften or melt the mixing container, char the resin, and produce noxious smoke and fumes. Because of this, some manufacturers place notices on their resin products, warning users that a large pot of curing resin can generate enough heat to ignite flammable materials that may be in the vicinity. Take this warning seriously! I have seen an entire composites shop evacuated by the toxic smoke generated from a poorly attended container of mixed resin. Once the smoke had cleared, scorch marks where found on the Formica tabletop where the container had been sitting. Needless to say, closely monitor the amount of time a mixed resin sits in its container because a large quantity of otherwise good resin can quickly go to waste if it is allowed to harden before being put to use in a molded composite.

Because of the amount of heat generated by mixed resin at different liquid volumes, resin manufacturers will list two cure speeds for their products: "pot life" and "working time". Pot life is the amount of time it takes the curing resin to begin gelling while sitting in a mixing container, such as a bucket or cup. This time can range from a couple minutes to several hours, depending on the resin system.

The working time of a resin refers to the amount of time a curing resin will remain liquid and usable while spread out into fabric reinforcements or in a mold before it begins to gel and varies from a few minutes to several hours. Keeping these times in mind, a wise fabricator will use a resin system that will provide enough working time to complete the layup before gelling starts, and then will only mix small, manageable amounts of resin at a time. For large jobs, it is helpful to have an assistant present to mix resin as needed for the layup. When an assistant is unavailable, it is beneficial to set out several cups of unmixed resin with several corresponding cups of properly measured catalyst or hardener — from these a new resin batch can be easily mixed as needed for the layup.

As a curing resin progresses toward full hardness, it goes through a gel stage that starts as the resin becomes thick and gelatinous, then hardening to a consistency of hard rubber. Some builders call this latter stage a "green cure". A green cured composite will still be flexible, but the laminate plies will be consolidated together. However, if the composite part is removed from the mold and deformed at this stage, it will continue to harden into that distorted shape. At this stage, the matrix can be damaged by rough cutting, pulling, or tearing of the laminate. It will still be somewhat delicate, and if sufficiently disturbed can begin to crumble into rubbery bits, destroying the effectiveness of the composite.

Photo 6: Polyester resin catalyst – MEKP. (Shown with an easy-to-use dispenser that has a built-in measuring cup.)

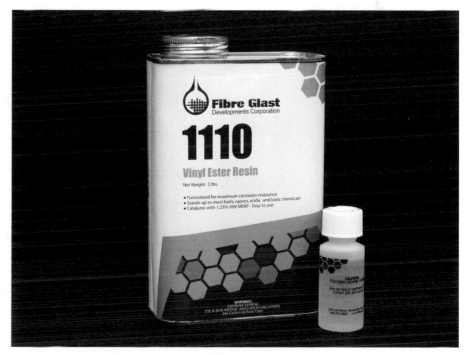

Photo 7: Vinylester resin – A reasonably priced alternative to polyester with good strength and chemical properties.

The time required for the resin to achieve a complete, solid cure is, again, dependent on the resin system, but can range from an hour to several days. The composite should remain in the mold until it has reached this solid cure state to avoid any deformation of the part's shape that may otherwise occur by removing it too soon. The solid cure time can often be accelerated by applying moderate heat to the composite or mold.

As a resin cures, it adheres most effectively to previously laminated plies in a layup if cross-linked chemical bonds can still be formed between the resin molecules. This is achievable when new resin and reinforcement plies are added to resin that is still wet, or at least tacky to the touch. However, if a resin is allowed to cure completely before the next layer is added, only an inferior secondary bond will form. With a secondary bond, the resin's adhesive strength is limited to how well it can solidify into the small scratches and surface imperfections of the previous cured layer. Secondary bonding, while sometimes required, should be avoided as much as possible in designing composites because they are generally more prone to delamination. We will discuss this topic more in Finishing Techniques chapter.

All resins naturally degrade when exposed to ultraviolet (UV) light. Over time, the energy in UV light breaks the chemical bonds in the resin's molecules, destroying its physical strength and ultimately rendering it into a useless powder. To combat this, some resins are enhanced with UV light inhibitors by the manufacturer. Other resins (such as epoxies) that can not necessarily be enhanced with such additives can still be protected from UV by applying special surface coatings or UV protective paints.

Another thing to keep in mind is that the resins used in composites act similarly to traditional adhesives. Like adhesives, the resins in composite laminates perform best in shear — or when they are resisting sliding motion between the fibers and layers of the laminate (see illustration 3). On the other hand, these resins tend to work least effectively in peel — or when the layers of the laminate are being pulled away from each other (see illustration 4). Composites that are subjected to excessive peel-like stresses may eventually succumb to delamination.

In recent years, various manufacturers have developed methods for increasing the peel strength between the laminate layers by developing special resins with higher peel strength, sewing the reinforcement layers together with additional fibers, or even weaving the fibers into three-dimensional shapes (somewhat like a robotic version of a knitting-needle-wielding grandmother) prior to adding the resin. However, high peel strength resins can be expensive, and most sewing or weaving methods require complex, specialized equipment that is generally out of the reach of the beginning composites builder.

One more resin property to consider is its viscosity, or its resistance to liquid flow. Thinner, or less viscous, resins will "wet-out" (or infiltrate) the fiber bundles in a woven reinforcement more easily because they are more liquid. Thicker, more viscous, resins will tend to help fill in the gaps between woven fiber bundles, minimizing voids in the composite because they will be less likely to soak into the fibers. Therefore, thin resins will spread into the fiber bundles of reinforcements

Photo 8: Epoxy resin – Highest cost with highest performance.

very quickly, but may require considerable final sanding to smooth out voids found on the surface between the fabric's weave. Conversely, thicker resins will be difficult to work into reinforcements during layup, but tend to produce much smoother, void-free final surfaces.

Because there are literally hundreds of polymer matrices available for use in composites, choosing one that is suitable for any given application can prove to be a daunting task. To simplify the selection process, this book will only focus on three of the most commonly used thermoset resin types: polyester, vinylester, and epoxy resins. Each of these is available at most hardware stores, automotive/body shop supply chains, composites suppliers, or other online sources. They are generally simple enough to use that the average fabricator can competently employ them in most projects.

POLYESTER RESIN

Polyester resin (see photo 5) is the most commonly used resin in mass-production and small composites shops, largely due to its relative low cost and adjustable cure time. It is regularly used by boating and bathtub/shower manufacturers, often with a protective coating called a "gel coat" — a pigmented or colored resin shell — also made of polyester resin. Polyester is very resistant to ultraviolet light and can be used where a composite's surfaces will be subjected to prolonged exposure in direct sunlight.

Polyester resin cures with the addition of a catalyst called MEKP (methyl ethyl keytone peroxide) — a chemical which assists the polyester molecules in cross-linking. Cure time can be controlled by adding more or less catalyst — more MEKP for short cure times, and less for longer cure times. Care should be taken to add the correct amount of catalyst for your needs, based upon the manufacturer's guidelines for the polyester resin. This is usually measured in drops of catalyst per ounce of resin, or by percentage of liquid volume as measured with a MEKP dispenser (see photo 6). If the resin has too little catalyst, it may never completely cure. However, if too much catalyst is added, it may cure pre-

maturely or otherwise generate so much heat that the resin becomes brittle once cured. With this in mind, though, properly measuring polyester resin and its catalyst is a simple task, especially when using mixing containers that have volume markings along with special MEKP dispensers.

Compared to other resins, polyester is relatively inexpensive. As of the printing of this book, prices for polyester resin range anywhere between $25 and $85 a gallon (and even less, when purchased in large quantities) depending on the resin's properties and additives. Laminating resins — used to build up multiple laminate layers — tend to be less expensive, but will leave a tacky surface on the resin for the bonding of subsequent layers. Surfacing, finishing, top coat, or "waxed" resins tend to be slightly more expensive but will produce a tack-free surface on the resin once cured because they will seal off oxygen from resin's surface, allowing it to cure completely.

Polyester resins are available in two basic chemical types: orthophthalic and isophthalic. These names refer to the actual orientation of the molecules in the polyester resin and have a large impact on the final cured resin's properties. For simplicity sake, though, orthophthalic resins tend to be a little less expensive and common in general-use layups. Isophthalic polyester resins

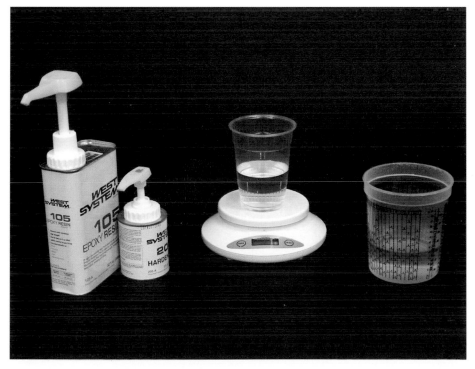

Photo 9: Epoxy can be measured in three ways: using manufacturer-supplied metering pumps (if available), weighing with a digital scale, or measuring liquid volume using a marked cup.

	Cost	Mechanical & Thermal Properties	Cure Time	V.O.C.	Cure Shrinkage	Best Used For...
Polyester Resin	Low	Low	Moderate to Fast (Limited Range)	High	High	General purpose, low-performance non-critical uses
Vinylester Resin	Moderate	Moderate	Moderate to Fast (Limited Range)	High	High	Special purpose, good performance non-critical uses
Epoxy Resin	Moderate to High	High	Slow to Fast	Low	Low	High-performance and safety-critical applications

Illustration 10: A simple comparison of the most common resins.

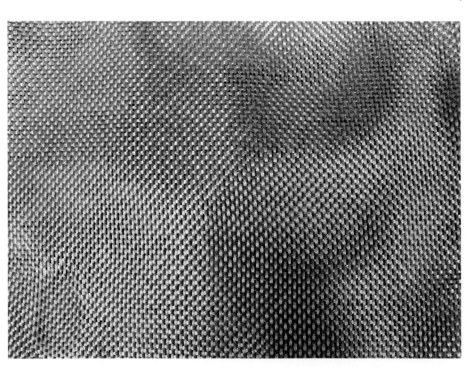

Photo 11: Fiberglass reinforcement – Low cost and good for general purpose use.

tend to have less shrinkage, higher strength and durability, and higher heat tolerance, so they are widely used in applications that require better performance.

One helpful property of polyester resins is that they have a low viscosity, making them easy to work into fabrics. They can also be thinned by simply mixing in additional styrene monomer (the chemical component that keeps the polyester resin liquid), even to the point of allowing it to be sprayed for some specialized layups. Styrene monomer will also help in extending the life of an otherwise old can of polyester resin that has begun to gel while in storage.

When compared to other resins, polyester tends to feel very tacky and sticky when wet. This is especially helpful in adhering reinforcements to vertical mold walls, but may cause frustration as polyester-wetted fibers will fasten to your hands and can quickly gum up your tools during layup.

Unfortunately, polyester tends to have some of the lowest strength of the common composite resins. Due, in part, to the high rate of shrinkage it experiences during curing — about a 7% volume reduction from its liquid form — stress is built up within the cured resin, taking away some of its overall useful strength. Even though reinforcements in the resin can help minimize this shrinkage, its strength is still somewhat compromised regardless. Because of its lower strength, it is not usually sensible to employ polyester resin with high performance fabrics, such as those employing carbon fibers. Polyester should also be avoided in use with aramid fabrics as it can have difficulty bonding with the fibers.

Another drawback of polyester resin is its dangerous volatile organic compound (VOC) vapor.

Polyester resin has a strong, penetrating odor very similar to that of automotive body fillers (in fact, most body fillers are polyester resin with thickening additives such as talc). The source of this smell is the styrene monomer in the polyester resin. Because of this styrene vapor, it is advisable to work with the polyester resin only in areas with adequate ventilation and while wearing a respirator (see the Health and Safety chapter for more information).

VINYLESTER RESIN

Vinylester resin is used by some builders instead of polyester resins due to its slightly higher performance (in some cases, approaching that of epoxy), excellent chemical resistance, ease of use, less water absorption than polyester, and excellent compatibility with polyester resins (See photo 7). With a cost between $40 to $80 per gallon and an MEKP controllable cure speed, vinylester can be an attractive option for applications that require better properties than those offered by polyester resin. For these reasons, vinylester is used in the production of high performance boat hulls and large chemical storage tanks. To attain these higher properties, though, it is generally necessary to perform post-cure heating of the vinylester, as directed by the manufacturer.

Vinylester resins can be more difficult to find than either polyester or epoxy resins, possibly because some individuals simply make a jump to epoxies if they need additional performance from their resin system. However, due to its similarity with polyester systems, vinylester could be considered an "upgrade" for fabricators who are familiar and comfortable with polyester resins. While it mixes and catalyzes the same as polyester, it provides additional strength and chemical resistance lacking in polyester resins.

Photo 12: Carbon fiber reinforcement — High strength and stiffness for high-performance use.

Photo 13: Aramid reinforcement — High strength and good abrasion resistance for high-performance and safety-critical applications.

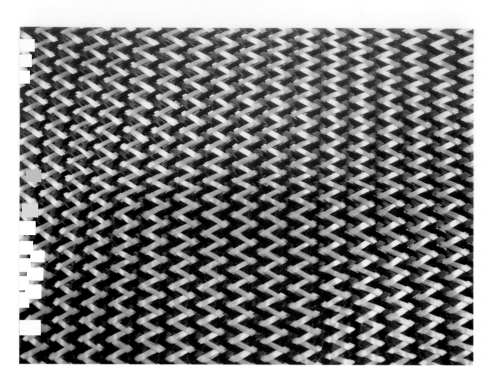

Photo 14: Hybrid reinforcement – Dissimilar reinforcements woven together for special properties in each fiber's direction.

	Cost	Weight	Laminate Rigidity	Laminate Impact Strength	Best Used For...
E-Glass	Low	Heavy	Flexible	Good	General purpose, non-critical parts and structures
S-Glass	Low to Moderate	Heavy	Flexible	Excellent	Special purpose, good performance structural uses
Carbon	High	Light	Stiff	Poor	High-performance high-stiffness structures
Aramid	Moderate	Moderate	Flexible	Excellent	High-strength ballistics/abrasion and safety uses
Hybrid	Moderate	Moderate	Flexible to Stiff	Good	Special purpose, good performance and aesthetic uses

Illustration 15: A simple comparison of the most common reinforcement types.

Unfortunately, also similar to polyester resin, vinylester shrinks considerably during cure, and likewise emits an unpleasant styrene monomer odor.

Vinylester is compatible with all reinforcement types, and is also more compatible with epoxy than polyester is. When polyester is used over a cured epoxy composite, it may not fully cure because of chemical interactions between the two resins. However, vinylester will generally cure well over either polyester or epoxy. Therefore, when making repairs or bonding to different resin types, vinylester resin can work well as a bonding interface between these disparate matrices.

EPOXY RESIN

Epoxy resins are used in applications where superior strength, durability, and chemical resistance are needed (see photo 8). Epoxies tend to be more expensive than either polyester or vinylester resins — ranging from $65 to over $180 a gallon — so cost should be considered in relation to the physical and chemical benefits epoxy can offer. Although epoxies can be used effectively with all fabric reinforcement types, they are especially well-suited for higher performance fabrics where their properties are most beneficial to the overall resulting composite.

Unlike the catalyzed reaction found in polyester and vinylester resins, epoxy resin cures through the addition of a hardener in a chemical reaction that actually cross-links the resin and hardener together. Whereas polyester and vinylester resins will simply harden faster when excess catalyst is added, epoxy's chemical reaction requires rather precise measurement of the resin and hardener components. This is to ensure that no excess liquid from either part is left over after the chemical reaction has completed and cause softening

22

or weakening of the final resin matrix. To guarantee proper mix ratios, some epoxy manufacturers supply special metering pumps that attach to the cans of each liquid component. Others advise measuring each part by weight — preferably with an accurate digital scale — or by volume using specially marked cups (see photo 9). Some aerospace epoxies even use a powdered form of hardener that is measured and mixed into the resin prior to layup.

Epoxy's physical properties depend heavily upon its chemical formulation, and can sometimes be enhanced by heating it after it has cured using special "post-cure" procedures designated by the manufacturer. These properties range from low to high strength, flexibility, heat, and chemical resistance and should be researched through the manufacturer's product information to find a good fit for your particular application prior to use. However, some general purpose resin systems are marketed by resin manufacturers specifically to do-it-yourself or small shop operations. Such resins often come with excellent support literature to help explain the uses and benefits of the particular epoxy resin system.

Epoxies are also available in varying viscosities, so consider the type of layup they are to be used in when shopping for a resin: low viscosity for resin transfer molding (an advanced layup method), low and medium viscosities for hand layup, and high viscosity for secondary bonding. Unfortunately, it is not advisable to thin epoxies with acetone or lacquer thinner because they will attack the chemical mechanisms that harden the epoxy, making it difficult or impossible for the epoxy to completely cure. Instead, some manufacturers suggest spreading the epoxy over the fabric reinforcement or area where it is to be used, and then warming it a bit with a heat gun to lower its viscosity. Even so, care should be taken when applying heat to the epoxy because it can speed up the cure time significantly.

One weakness of epoxy is that it can degrade in the presence of UV light. While UV-resistant versions of both polyester and vinylester resins are readily available, epoxy resins require alternative protection methods — such as special surface coatings — to protect them from UV damage. Such methods will be discussed in the section on Finishing Techniques.

Lastly, epoxy resins generally have very low VOC vapors, usually alleviating the need for special respirators. However, they can produce allergic reactions in some people, especially if the epoxy or hardener comes in contact with the skin. Even individuals who show no initial signs of allergy to these liquids can actually become more sensitive to them over time. To minimize the allergic effects of epoxies, follow the precautions listed in this book's chapter on Health and Safety.

The following chart shows a simple comparison of these various resins based on their relative cost, mechanical and thermal properties, cure time, V.O.C., and cure shrinkage (see illustration 10).

REINFORCEMENT TYPES AND PROPERTIES

Just as there are several resin types available for use in composites, different reinforcement fibers with a variety of strength properties are also available. Fiber reinforcements come in a few different material types, each with its own special properties and price affixed to it. Some of these include the previously mentioned fiberglass, as well as carbon (or graphite), aramid, hybrids, and other less commonly used specialty fibers.

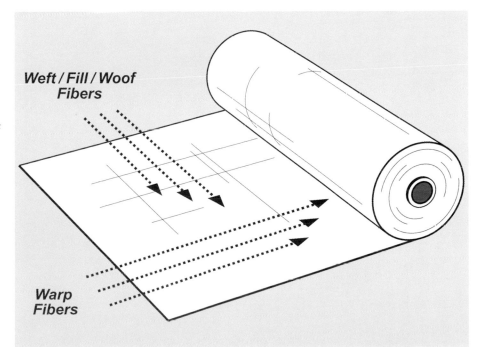

Illlustration 16: "Warp" yarns run the length of the woven fabric; "Weft", "fill", and "woof" yarns (all names use interchangeably in the textile industry) run the width of the fabric.

Illustration 17: Plain weave – A simple over-and-under weave style.

FIBERGLASS

Fiberglass is the most common reinforcement used in composites, largely due to its low cost and availability (see photo 11). Recreational watercraft, such as boats and jet skis, use fiberglass extensively in their hulls. Likewise, the automotive and transportation industries have utilized fiberglass reinforcements in the construction of vehicles for decades, ranging from passenger and sports cars to buses, light-rail, and semi-truck bodies. Fiberglass is common even in the aerospace industry for various aircraft structures, especially for small and home-built aircraft designs which use it extensively for molding entire airplane bodies.

Fiberglass comes in a few different grades, the two most common of which are "E-glass" and "S-glass". E-glass is an economical, electrical-grade, general-use fiberglass common in marine, architecture, and automotive applications. S-glass is high performance fiberglass that has over 25% more strength than E-glass and is used in aerospace, engineering, and racing.

Some vendors also offer fiberglass in a variety or colors. These colors come from the "sizing", or special coatings used during manufacture, deposited on the glass filaments rather than as color additives within the glass itself.

CARBON FIBER

Carbon fiber is an especially sought-after reinforcement because of its low weight, high strength, and stiffness characteristics (see photo 12). It has been used very heavily in the aerospace industry for decades, but in recent years has found its way into racing, automotive, industrial, and recreational goods. It is more expensive than most other fibers, but the cost difference is usually justified where superior performance is required.

In addition to its excellent strength characteristics, carbon

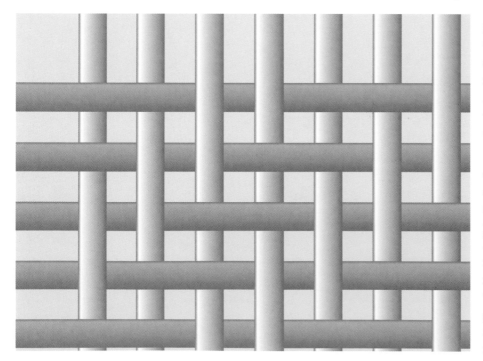

Illustration 18: Twill weave – Each yarn travels over-two and under-two other yarns.

fiber has workability and aesthetic qualities that set it apart from other composites. Carbon fabrics generally lay into a mold with less effort than fiberglass of the same weight and can be cut and sanded more cleanly and easily using common tools than either fiberglass or aramid fibers. Many composites fabricators mention that they prefer its workability over either fiberglass or aramid.

Although carbon fiber comes only in black — though some vendors erroneously sell dyed aramid fibers as "colored carbon" — it has a unique aesthetic that makes it an attractive choice for unpainted or visible composites. When impregnated with resin, fiberglass tends to have a slightly brownish green or purple translucency to it, while an aramid fibers' color tends to appear dulled and muted. Carbon fiber, however, produces a look of woven black silk. Its light reflections seem to trick the eye, creating a somewhat holographic effect with the fibers. The most interesting light patterns tend to come with twill weave carbon — making it highly sought after by fabricators who want to show off the carbon fiber in their projects.

"Commercial" and "aerospace" grades of carbon fiber are available with varying ranges of strength associated to them. For most applications, though, home composites builders tend to find that commercial grades are less expensive and more easily obtained than aerospace grades — while still filling their project's strength and weight requirements. However, while some fabricators may use the terms "carbon" and "graphite" interchangeably, true graphite fibers have higher strength characteristics than do typical carbon fibers.

Carbon fiber's fabric weight is often measured in terms of a how many 1000's of filaments are found in a fiber bundle — expressed in

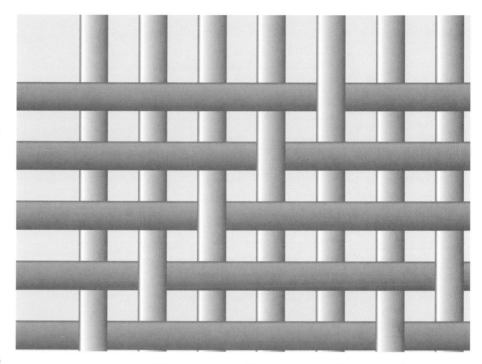

Illustration 19: Satin weave – Yarns travel over-one and under-multiple yarns in this weave.

Illustration 20: Basket weave – Similar to a plain weave, but with two yarns traveling under-and-over two yarns at a time.

25

	Weave Stability	Wet-out	Drape	Best Used For...
Plain Weave	Excellent	Good	Poor	High-performance flat or low-curvature shapes
Twill Weave	Good	Good	Good	Good-performance medium-curvature shapes
Satin Weave	Poor	Poor	Excellent	General purpose high-curvature shapes
Basket Weave	Good	Excellent	Poor	Good-performance flat or low-curvature shapes

Illustration 21: A simple comparison of some common weave styles.

Photo 22: Yarns woven together to form a tube-like structure are called "sock", "sleeve", or "tubing".

"K". For example, 1K fabric would have 1000 filaments per fiber bundle whereas 3K would have 3000 filaments. 3K, 6K, 12K, and 24K are common filament counts. 3K fabrics are used for typical layups, 6K fabrics for quick build up of a laminate, and 12K and 24K are employed in creating composite tooling (also known as tooling fabrics) such as molds. As with other available fabrics, carbon fiber is also specified by weight per square yard and by thickness.

ARAMID FIBER

Named from a shortened version of its chemical name ("aromatic polyamide"), aramid fiber is very lightweight, strong, abrasion resistant, heat resistant, and non-conductive (see photo 13). These characteristics make it especially useful in composites that will be employed in tough environments or where safety is crucial. Aramid fiber is naturally yellow in color and is commonly available under the DuPont brand name "Kevlar". It is available in three grades: Kevlar (as a reinforcement in rubber goods), Kevlar-29 (for general industrial and armor use), and Kevlar-49 (for high-performance and transportation applications).

With its many benefits, aramid fibers also have some unique qualities that make them difficult to use. They are notoriously difficult to cut and will tend to become stringy and fray instead of simply shearing if you use even slightly dulled scissors. In a cured composite this resistance to cutting becomes notably troublesome as it is very difficult to trim an aramid composite and still produce a clean edge. For this reason, some manufacturers employ abrasive water-jet cutting equipment or specialty cutting bits to cleanly carve through their cured aramid parts.

Take care in using aramid fiber in the presence of ultraviolet light. When dyed, aramid fibers return to their natural yellow color after prolonged UV exposure. After considerable time in UV light, aramid fiber will begin to turn brown and lose its strength. To protect it from such degradation, use UV protective coatings and surface treatments.

HYBRID FIBER WEAVES

Hybrid weaves are created by interlacing two different reinforcement types, such as carbon and aramid, or carbon and fiberglass. These weaves also create a unique aesthetic, especially when dyed aramid fiber is used in the weave along with carbon or fiberglass.

For applications that need different strength characteristics in multiple directions, hybrid weaves are especially useful (see photo 14,). For instance, prosthetics use hybrids where good stiffness is needed in one direction, but flexibility in is desired in another.

A chart showing a generalized comparison of the most common reinforcement types is found in Illustration 15. As there are several different physical aspects related to the actual strength characteristics of any given reinforcement, refer to the "Additional Readings and Resources" section for more technical resources.

OTHER FIBER TYPES

Just as there are continual developments in resin chemistries, reinforcements are constantly being improved and developed. Other specialty fiber types that are worth exploring as you build with composites include the following:

- Dyneema - A form of ultra high molecular weight (UHMW) polyethylene fiber. It has excellent resistance to moisture, chemicals, and impact, along with good electrical and antiballistic properties.

- Zylon - A synthetic fiber with properties similar to Kevlar. It has excellent strength and thermal stability.

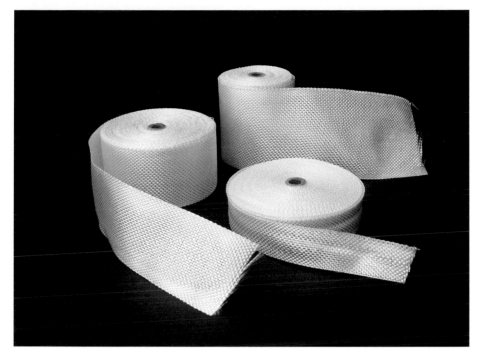

Photo 23: "Tapes" come in different narrow widths and resemble typical woven cloth.

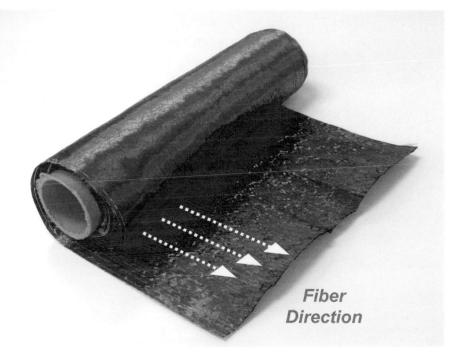

Fiber Direction

Photo 24: Produced so reinforcement fibers are traveling mainly in one direction, "unidirectional" fabric is excellent for optimized strength and smooth-surfaced composites.

- Aluminized Fiberglass – Woven fiberglass with a shiny, ultra-thin coating of aluminum that has been vapor-deposited on it. Originally produced to dissipate lightning strikes on composite aircraft, it has a unique "woven metal" aesthetic that produces interesting visual effects.

- Colored and Black Fiberglass – Available in a variety of colors for special aesthetic applications. Black fiberglass is sometimes used as a lower-cost alternative to mimic carbon fiber's aesthetic.

- Quartz – Another alternative to fiberglass with higher strength and stiffness, lower density, and nearly zero expansion or contraction over a wide range of temperatures.

- Basalt – An inexpensive alternative to fiberglass with even better chemical resistance than glass.

- Boron – A very light fiber with excellent stiffness and strength. It is created by vapor-depositing boron onto carbon or tungsten filaments. Though it is often used in aerospace for applications that require extreme performance, some high-end consumer goods utilize it as well.

Several other fiber types are also available, but it is advisable to experiment with a small sample of any new reinforcement you intend to use prior to applying it in your particular laminate application. Regardless of the reinforcement type, it is supplied in a range of woven patterns and fiber weights, including specialty non-woven types.

Photo 25: "Mat" fabrics are comprised of randomly arranged short fibers held together with a special binder.

Woven reinforcements are made from filaments that are bundled and woven into fabric. The individual filaments used in fiber reinforcement can range in thicknesses from about the coarseness of horsehair to finer than a baby's hair. In order to be easily woven, these filaments are gathered into bundles called tow or roving, or into twisted bundles called "yarns". These bundles are then woven together using industrial textile equipment to create either of two types of fabric: woven roving or cloth (made from woven yarn). Since they are made of thick filament bundles, woven roving reinforcements tend to come in heavier weights and accept more resin during layup due to the inherent spacing between the filaments. Conversely, the tightly bundled filaments in cloth tend to fray less and create slightly thinner fabrics that use less resin.

Woven reinforcements are designated and sold in terms of the fabric's thickness (in inches), "weight" — frequently measured in ounces per square yard — and by the number of "warp" yarns (those that travel the length of the cloth roll) and "weft", "fill", or "woof" yarns (those that travel the width of the cloth) per inch of fabric (see illustration 16). For example, a particular fiberglass cloth may be measured as .0093" thick, weighing 8.8 ounces per yard, with a warp count of 54 yarns per inch, and a fill count of 18 yarns per inch.

The pattern of a reinforcement's weave will affect its directional strength, ability to be wetted with resin, how much resin it can hold, the final surface quality of the composite, and its "drapeability" — or how well it will conform to complex mold shapes. Some common weave types include plain, twill, satin, and basket. Additional specialty weaves such as sock/sleeve/tubing and tapes are also available.

PLAIN WEAVE

This weave style is the most common among the common fabric reinforcement types (see illustration 17). It is produced by weaving each warp and fill fiber in a simple over-one and under-one pattern. This particular weave produces a stable fabric that is easily wetted with resin. Additionally, either side of the fabric is very symmetrical, allowing it to spread stresses more evenly amongst its fibers.

Some drawbacks of this weave include its uneven surface and poor drape. Because its fiber bundles pass over and under each other so closely, this weave style tends to cause crimping in the fibers. Such crimping can produce small, regularly patterned pores in the surface of a cured laminate where the fibers are unable to securely lay against the mold's face. This crimping effect is especially pronounced in heavier fabrics — relegating a plain weave's use primarily to lighter fabrics. Also, as plain woven fibers experience such a tight orientation in the weave, they have less ability to slide over each other to accommodate large, complex curves when molded. For this reason, plain weave is most commonly used in flat or planar-shaped composite parts.

TWILL WEAVE

Twill weaves tend to have the best combination of drapeability and strength (see illustration 18). Because of this, it is widely used in applications that require both good formability and high performance. Additionally, twill tends to produce a very desirable aesthetic, especially with carbon fabrics. A very common configuration of this weave is a 2/2 twill in which a warp fiber goes over and under two fill fibers.

SATIN WEAVE

Satin weaves offer exceptional formability, but at the expense of having some of the lowest stability (see illustration 19). Due to its weave pattern, it tends to fray very easily when applied in a wet layup, so use care when moving the fabric around after cutting it. "5-harness" (where the fibers go over-one and under-five) and "crowfoot" are common styles for this type of weave.

BASKET WEAVE

Basket weaves are very similar to plain weaves except that they will use two or more fiber bundles to go over and under two or more other fiber bundles at a time (see illustration 20). They tend to lay flatter than other weaves but are prone to fraying more than a typical plain weave.

The chart in illustration 21 shows a quick comparison of the most common weave styles based on the fiber stability in the weave,

its ability to be wet with resin, and its drapeability .

Aside from typical woven cloth, other reinforcement forms are available, depending on the needs of a particular composite application. Some of these include sock, sleeve, or tubing, tapes, and even non-woven varieties.

SOCK/SLEEVE/TUBING

The names "sock", "sleeve", or "tubing" are all synonymous for a specialty form of fabric that comes in a continuous tube, resembling a sock or sleeve (see photo 22). It is created by spirally interlacing a plain weave of yarns fed from spools of reinforcement fibers. When compressed about its length, the diameter increases. Conversely, when stretched, the sock's diameter decreases — similar to novelty finger-cuffs.

This flexibility in diameter and length is helpful in fabricating tubular structures, including those that change in shape along their length — such as handlebars or aesthetic exhaust tubing.

TAPES

Some specialty reinforcements come woven into narrow "tapes" that resemble their wider fabric counterparts (see photo 23). They come in different widths ranging from 1 to 10 inches and are available in most common reinforcement fiber types. These tapes are especially useful for localized or directional reinforcement of a laminate. Since they can be used by simply cutting the tape to length, they are less prone to fray-

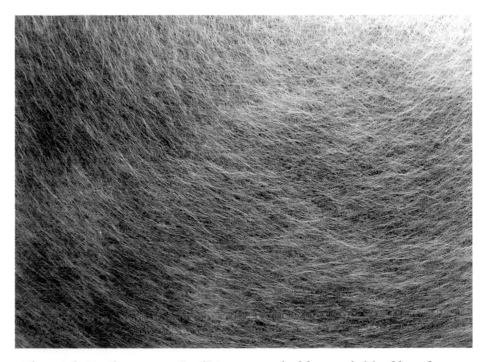

Photo 26: Similar to mat, "veil" is composed of fine, web-like fibers for specialty application.

Photo 27: "Tow" is a reinforcement yarn that comes on spools and is primarily used for filament winding applications.

ing than other fabrics and are especially helpful when working on small layups and projects.

Non-woven Reinforcements are used for composite laminates that require special properties uncommon in woven reinforcements. Some of these properties include added strength through very controlled, directional fiber alignment or added bulk with multidirectional fiber placement. To achieve these ends, unidirectional fiber, mat, veil, and tow, strand, or roving are available.

Unidirectional Fiber

For applications that require maximum strength per volume, unidirectional fiber, or "uni", is an excellent option (see photo 24). Unidirectional fiber is created by orienting all of the fibers of the reinforcement in one direction, then using a light binder or periodic woven fill fibers to loosely hold the reinforcements together. Unidirectional fiber comes wound on rolls and will lie very flat to form tight, void free laminates. This characteristic is very desirable for mass-production parts because it requires less surface preparation to remove pin-holes and voids prior to painting or surface coating. However, In spite of their excellent strength and fiber consolidation, unidirectional composites tend to delaminate more easily than those created with woven fabrics because there are no significant fill yarns tying the warp fibers in place.

Mat

Supplied in rolls, and used for multi-directional strength and quick build-up of the laminate, "mat" is composed of randomly arranged short fibers held together by a special binder (see photo 25). Mat is used extensively for marine and automotive body repair. Though it has good multi-directional strength, mat has large gaps between the fibers that tend to harbor excess resin, creating a relatively heavy and brittle composite.

Photo 28: Fiberglass bundles on a spool are called "roving" and are widely used with copper guns for spray-ups.

VEIL

As a laminate is heated or exposed to wet environments, the resin and fibers within it may expand and contract slightly. When this happens, a phenomenon called "print through" occurs, showing off a faint image of the fiber weave in the surface of the laminate. To minimize print through, some builders will use a layer of "veil" prior to layup of woven fabrics. Veil is a very thin fabric with a cobweb-like appearance (see photo 26). It is very similar to mat in its makeup, containing randomly oriented fibers with a binder, but is composed of much finer fibers than mat. Similarly to mat fabrics, veil will accept excessive amounts of resin, and is therefore rarely used alone in a composite.

TOW/STRAND/ROVING

When reinforcements are supplied as fibers bundled on reels, they are referred to as "tow", "strand", or "roving" (see photo 27). High-performance fibers, such as carbon and aramid, are typically supplied as "tow" or "strand" and are commonly used in filament winding processes. Filament winding produces pressure vessels and specialty structures that have incredible strength through specific, directed — and usually automated — fiber alignment.

Fiberglass filaments, gathered together as "roving", are also used in filament winding, but are mostly utilized in spray layups with a chopper gun (see photo 28). This form of fiberglass is available in large bulk spools, often sold in large boxes that feed the roving out from the center of the spool into the chopper gun.

In most cases, reinforcements can be easily cut with sharp scissors or a rotary fabric cutter (see photo 29). Finely serrated, or all metal, scissors tend to work well with most reinforcement fabrics. When cutting aramids, a pair of very sharp, short-bladed scissors work best.

CHAPTER CONCLUSION

Thermoset resins come in several types, three of which include polyester, vinylester, and epoxy resins. Likewise, fiber reinforcements come in several fiber types in multiple woven and non-woven styles. When designating materials for a composite, it is important to consider the cost, use, and specific properties of these different materials.

Photo 29: Most reinforcements can be easily cut with sharp scissors. Finely serrated and all-metal scissors tend to work best.

Chapter Three

Health and Safety

Maintaining a Safe Work Environment

Cured composites present very few health hazards other than dust particles they can produce. However, typical of many liquid chemicals, you should use resins and solvents with care to protect yourself from unhealthy exposure. You should be particularly aware of safeguarding your eyes, ears, and lungs, as well as any exposed skin.

GENERAL HEALTH CONCERNS WITH COMPOSITES

As with any building materials — especially those that use liquid chemicals or produce dust — there are a few guidelines that should be adhered to when using composites in order to ensure safe construction. The following include specific health and safety concerns

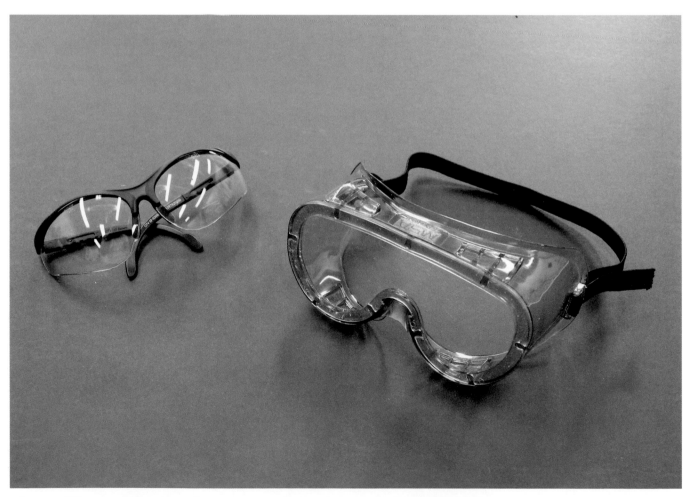

Photo 1: Wear eye protection whenever using chemicals or in the presence of dust.

associated with composites to avoid uncomfortable, unhealthy, or life-threatening situations. While the following guidelines may be familiar to anyone who has spent any respectable length of time in a shop or manufacturing environment, they should be taken seriously to avoid uncomfortable or dangerous situations related to vision, hearing, breathing, or skin contact.

VISION

Eye protection should be worn anytime liquid chemicals are used or airborne dust is present in the composites work environment (see photo 1). This simple protection will help protect you from any inadvertent chemical splashes, including those from resins or cleaning agents. Likewise, eye protection can prevent any dangerous particles from irritating or lodging in the eyes, especially when power tools are being used to trim composites.

Goggles made specifically for use with chemicals will provide the most protection from chemical splashes as they cover the face and eyes from all sides. However, if chemicals do come in contact with the eyes, flush them immediately with water and consult a physician.

HEARING

Power tools used for cutting and sanding tend to create noise levels that can damage hearing sensitivity through repeated or prolonged exposure. To avoid hearing loss, use adequate ear protection, such as in-ear plugs or sound-deadening earmuffs (see photo 2) anytime power tools or other loud equipment are in use.

BREATHING

Airborne dust created by trimming a composite can be especially dangerous to your lungs. This is true not only of larger particles created when cutting composites, but also by the fine dust generated by sanding composites. Whenever possible, use a fine par-

ticle mask to minimize inhalation of dust (see photo 3). Dust can be significantly reduced by using some of the wet-sanding techniques included in the Finishing Techniques chapter.

Even though they may seem rather innocuous, raw fabrics can present breathing hazards of their own. When cut, reinforcement fabrics will produce small fiber pieces that can become airborne. Protect yourself from these stray fibers by using a dust mask while cutting and patterning fabrics.

Exposure to chemical fumes, such as those present when using polyester and vinylester resins and solvents, should be lessened by using a snugly fitting NIOSH (National Institute for Occupational Safety and Health) respirator with fresh organic vapor filters. Without such a helpful breathing aid, light-headedness and nausea may quickly occur. As an added means of decreasing exposure to chemical fumes, always ensure good ventilation when around liquid resins. Use an electric fan, such as a large box fan, as needed to bring fresh air into your work area.

SKIN CONTACT

Although there is not much chemical danger when skin comes in contact with a cured composite, uncured resins may have serious effects on a person's health,

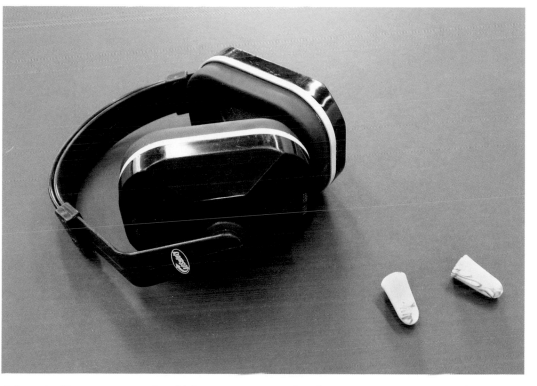

Photo 2: Ear protection should be worn anytime loud equipment or power tools are in use.

especially related to their allergies. This is particularly true of epoxies and the allergic sensitization they can cause, as previously mentioned. To ensure the safe handling of these liquids, use latex gloves (or nitrile gloves, if you are allergic to latex) on your hands whenever touching liquid or partially cured resins (see photo 4). Special barrier creams made specifically for use with resins can provide added protection as well. Not only will these help you avoid skin reactions, but will also help in clean-up after a layup is complete. If, in spite of adhering to these precautions, you do experience an allergic reaction to epoxy, immediately discontinue its use.

Special care should also be taken when handling MEKP catalysts, as they can cause burns to the skin. If a spill does occur, completely wash the skin with water as soon as possible.

Avoid getting resin on other areas of your body. Exposed arms are often the most difficult to shield but it is important to protect them as well because redness and itching can quickly develop on the sensitive skin found at the soft under-part of your forearms once in contact with resin. If you do get resin on your skin, do not use solvent to remove it; doing so will simply thin out the resin and allow it to penetrate your skin and migrate into your bloodstream. Instead, wipe off as much resin as possible with an absorbent paper towel or rag, then use strong soap (such as any citrus-based cleaner commonly found in automotive stores) and warm water to remove the remaining resin residue.

When trimming or cutting a cured composite, protect your skin from rough or sharp edges which may cause scratches, abrasions, and heinous slivers, by wearing leather gloves, like those common to sheet metal working. Fiberglass and carbon fiber pieces can be extremely stiff, so use caution whenever near exposed strands or fibers. If stray composite slivers lodge in your skin, simply extract them with tweezers. Apply a common antiseptic, such as rubbing alcohol or hydrogen peroxide, to the sliver site and use a bandage to prevent infection.

The fine particles produced during trimming and sanding can also cause considerable irritation as their stiff microscopic fibers lodge in the skin. Some individuals find success in avoiding such familiar itchy scenarios by either wearing a long sleeved shirt, closing their pores with a gratuitous application of talcum powder prior to working, or by rinsing their skin with very hot water to sweat the fibers out from their pores.

OTHER CONCERNS

As with any industrial chemicals, the resins, catalysts, hardeners, or solvents used with composites should not be ingested. If such a mishap occurs, follow the chemical manufacturer's recommendations and seek immediate medical assistance.

Uncured resins present an additional flammability hazard that must be considered and conscientiously accommodated. Store resins away from any heat sources, including space heaters, open flame shop heaters, water

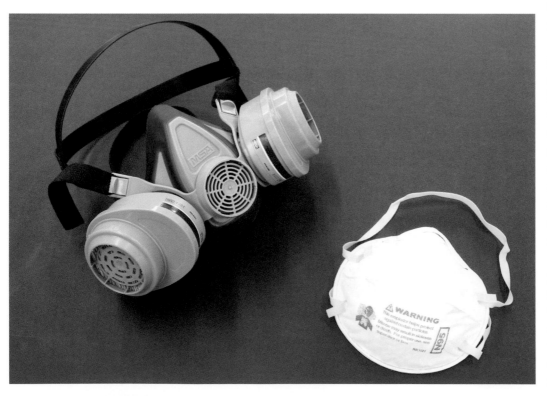

Photo 3: Use a NIOSH approved respirator when using high V.O.C. chemicals. Wear a dust mask to avoid inhaling fine particles or fibers.

heaters, furnaces, and lit cigarettes. Solvents can be even more dangerous as their vapors can often be heavier than air, posing potential fire hazards around pilot lights and other flame sources. Always ensure that all liquid chemicals used with composites are properly contained, stored, and then used in a well-ventilated, ignition-source free environment. Dispose of resin and solvent-soaked rags in a fire-safe waste receptacle.

On a smooth concrete or tile floor, spilled liquid resins can be as slick as the proverbial banana peel. They can also create a difficult clean-up problem if tracked all over a work space. To avoid any potential problems, wipe up spilled chemicals as quickly as possible with absorbent paper or cloth rags, or with absorbent sand, sawdust, wood chips, or cat litter.

In addition to these general health and safety concerns, beware of resin contact with clothing or tools. Inadvertently smearing or dripping resin on expensive or important objects can cause costly damage. Wear appropriate work clothing when fabricating composites, such as an old t-shirt, thick but comfortable jeans, and shoes. Even though shorts may be tempting to wear while working with composites in warm weather, it would be wise to put on pants instead. If resin drops into one's leg hair, or if jagged-edged parts rub against your legs it can cause some very unpleasant or painful problems.

CHAPTER CONCLUSION

Liquid chemicals and dusts provide the most common health and safety dangers with composites. Wear eye protection when using chemicals and power tools. Also use ear protection around power tools. Use a dust mask when working around dust, and wear an approved respirator when using vapor-producing chemicals. Avoid contact with liquids and abrasive composites by using gloves. For additional safety, do not use chemicals around heat sources, immediately wipe up spills, and wear suitable work clothing.

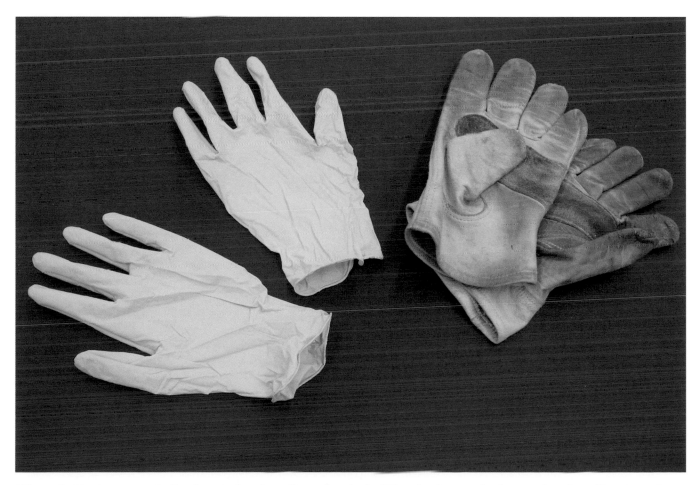

Photo 4: Use latex or nitrile gloves when handling chemicals. Wear leather work gloves when handling jagged-edged composites.

Chapter Four

Setting Up Shop

Materials, Chemicals, and Tools of the Trade

As with any metal or wood shop, a composites shop needs its own space and special equipment. Shop space should include adequate temperature control, ventilation, and space. Equipment used in the fabrication of composites mainly consists of tools commonly available at most hardware or home-improvement stores, although some special-ty items can only be acquired from composites suppliers.

SHOP SPACE

Fabricating a composite requires special work-space considerations. Resins cure best within specific temperature ranges, they can often produce fumes, and they can be extremely messy to use.

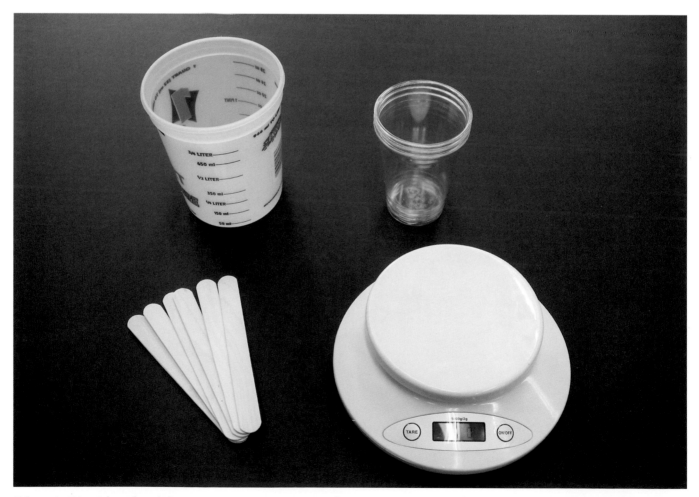

Photo 1: Liquid and weight measuring equipment and common mixing sticks are a must when working with resins.

Additionally, the performance of the composite depends upon the cleanliness of the environment and the materials used. To ensure an optimal workspace for composites fabrication, take the following guidelines into consideration.

Composites should be created in a room that has a controlled, stable temperature for the duration of the layup and cure cycle. Most resin systems work best at room-temperature, around 75 degrees Fahrenheit. However if there is any variation in your work area's temperature, it is best if it errs to the side of warmth rather than cold. Cold resin will cure painfully slow, or may simply not cure at all. Warm resin, though, will cure faster than normal, and will at least likely cure completely. Fabricators in warm climates routinely operate with their doors open to the outside air without problems. However, in cold climates, shop temperature control is imperative.

As mentioned earlier, polyester and vinylester resins can be hazardous to breathe for prolonged periods of time, and solvent fumes are generally dangerous in their own right. Even epoxy resins can cause fume hazards if they are allowed to overheat — as with an unattended mixed pot gone awry (as previously mentioned). A well ventilated work area will keep noxious vapors to a minimum. Whenever possible, open windows to promote positive airflow from outside, or otherwise facilitate adequate ventilation with dedicated fume hoods and ductwork, fans, or open-air workspaces.

Photo 2: For cutting reinforcements and preparing mold surfaces, a variety of cutting tools and aerosol sprayers are helpful.

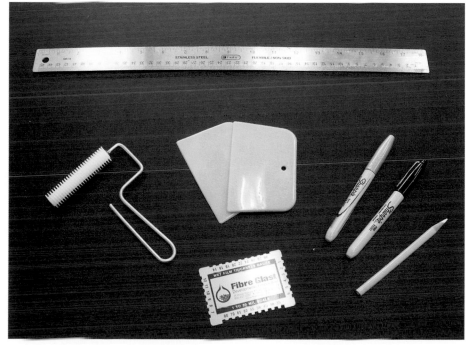

Photo 3: Rulers and markers are great for marking reinforcements before cutting, and rollers and spreaders help to work resin into reinforcement fabrics. A gel coat gauge shows the thickness of a resin gel or surface coat.

In order to produce a high-quality laminate, a composites workspace should have minimal dust or contaminants and be otherwise well organized and clean. This is a far cry from the typical woodworking or metal shop, but is nonetheless very important. Dust, debris, foreign chemicals, water, and other matter can compromise the resin's adhesion within the composite. These impurities can cause surface blistering and delamination in the final laminate, and can make the composite appear very sloppy. To ensure good fabrication results, minimize dust in your workspace by, at the very least, hanging painters' drop cloths or polyethylene plastic sheeting as room dividers to keep unwanted dust and other matter out. Such a precaution is of utmost importance when doing surfacing coats on a composite to produce a high luster surface for a completed part.

To further guarantee a clean composites environment, it is best to dedicate at least two distinctly separate work spaces in your shop: one for layups, and one for various mold-making and finishing tasks. These spaces should be adequately isolated from each other with walls or hanging drop cloths. Layups always work best in a clean environment. This includes the layup of composite molds and the application of final resin surface coats as well. However, roughing out a mold plug, part trimming, and typical sanding procedures can generate unmanageable amounts of dust. Isolating these activities from each other will markedly improve the overall quality of your composite fabrication endeavors.

Space organization and general cleanliness are extremely helpful in maintaining the dust-free, clean environment needed for composites. The less organization a composites workspace has, the more difficult it will be to fabricate in it. Make generous amounts of easily accessible shelf space available to organize tools and materials. Likewise, arrange your workspace so it is free of cumbersome obstacles, unnecessary items, and tight

Photo 4: A variety of common hand tools, along with some good shaping rasps, are invaluable in building molds and moldless parts.

spaces. A complicated layup is far less frustrating when you are not stumbling over car parts, pets, or garage-sale fodder.

One mistake many fabricators make is to underestimate the amount of space needed for composites work. This is especially true of table or workbench space. Mold prep, cutting, layup, demolding, and other tasks require considerable room. As a general rule of thumb, the tabletop area required to perform a layup alone is at least three to five times the size of the parts you are planning to form. In addition to space for layups, provide room for sizing and cutting reinforcement fabrics. Typically, the area of a 4' x 8' table top will suffice for this unless you are embarking on a project outside the scope of a reasonably-sized wet layup. Again, it is advisable to have separate tables for cutting and layup to avoid unwanted resin spills onto clean reinforcement fabrics. Lastly, if possible, set your work surfaces at a height that will be comfortable to lean or stand over for extended periods of time. Squatting too low or lifting your arms too high for an hour or two at a time can cause considerable fatigue.

Make sure you have sufficient lighting in your work area. Even if the only space you have available is in the tool shed behind the hydrangea bush, set up some overhead utility lights or other lighting to illuminate your work area. Ample light will help you avoid dangerous obstacles, inadvertent chemical spills, or poorly applied laminate plies.

When finding a location to perform composite fabrication, try to avoid the "ship-in-a-bottle" mistake. It is often hard to visualize the actual dimensions and sheer size of a large project unless you exercise some foresight and plan ahead. Piece-by-piece construction can quickly cause problems if your project begins to outgrow its ability to fit through the door. Though it may seem like common sense, make sure you've planned for a way to move your final composite out of the shop once it is completed.

Photo 5: A few different saws are helpful for cutting anything from mold-building materials to final composite laminates.

Basic Composites Layup Tools

There are several tools and materials used in the fabrication of composites that are somewhat specialized and difficult to find. However, the majority of what is needed to form composites is readily available at the local hardware store, and may already be in your shop. In some instances, as noted, inexpensive substitutes can be used to perform the same tasks. (See photos 1 through 17.)

Measuring and mixing containers

General use measuring and mixing containers are available at most paint and hardware stores. For just mixing, though, "recycled" and well-cleaned plastic tubs (from butter or other grocery items) can be equally effective.

Mixing sticks

To mix resins thoroughly (and cleanly), popsicle sticks, tongue suppressors, or paint mixing sticks all work very well. Before mixing, be sure there are no stray wood splinters or splits in the mixing stick that may find their way into the resin.

Digital scale

Nowadays, a good digital scale can be purchased for considerably less than just a few years ago. For small resin batches, invest in a scale that can precisely measure small quantities, such as one that is accurate to 1/10th of a gram. For large batches, a larger scale can be helpful.

Scissors

Do not underestimate the importance of a pair of sharp, high-quality scissors. All-metal scissors will provide the best service as well as the ability to be re-sharpened once dull. They are available at upholstery supply shops and cost a bit extra, but are well worth the investment. If your shop budget is tight, at least get scissors that have all-metal blades — plastic-reinforced blades will not last long against the coarse, thick fabrics used in composites. If you intend to build with aramid fabrics, obtain a pair of scissors that have serrated blades made of high carbon steel.

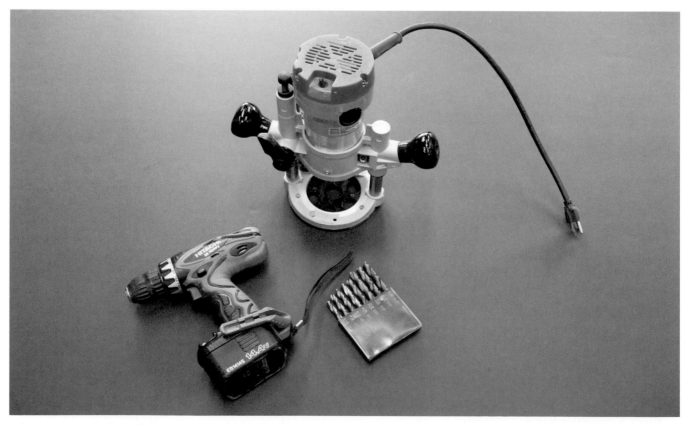

Photo 6: For drilling holes and routing edges of molding materials, use a good drill and router with high quality bits.

AIRBRUSH

A small hobby airbrush is helpful in applying liquid mold-release evenly to mold surfaces. Some airbrush kits come with a small compressor and air tank, but can run off a shop's air compressor line if used with a regulator (15 psi is generally enough pressure to get good coverage with the mold-release).

REFILLABLE AEROSOL SPRAY KIT

Some manufacturers make small aerosol spray paint kits that contain a pressurize air can with a detachable and refillable bottle. These work well for those who want to avoid investing in an air-brush to apply liquid mold-release. Make sure to clean it out after each use by spraying water through it, since it may otherwise clog or cause spray spatters.

UTILITY KNIFE

A simple utility knife can be used for cutting tapes, films, and other items. It is also helpful in cutting thick, heavy reinforcements when guided with a metal-edged ruler.

ROTARY CUTTER

Rotary cutters are available at fabric stores and are good for cutting thin fiberglass and carbon fiber reinforcements. The blades are replaceable, and circle-cutting attachments are available for them as well.

METAL-EDGED RULER

When cutting straight lines in reinforcement fabrics, a durable metal-edged ruler is very helpful.

SPREADERS

Commonly used in automotive bodywork, simple plastic spreaders are great for spreading resin into flat reinforcements. Once the resin has cured on them it can be easily removed with a quick flex of the spreader.

RESIN ROLLERS

To help consolidate composites and work extra-tacky resins into reinforcements — such as polyester resin and fiberglass composites — these ringed rollers work very well. Disposable types and

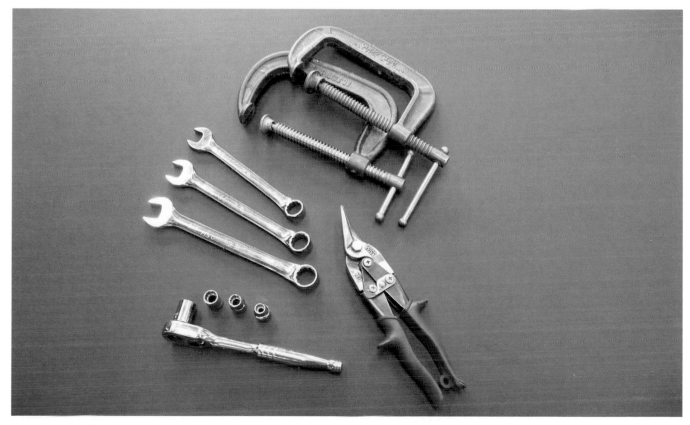

Photo 7: Additional helpful hand tools include clamps, metal snips, sockets, and wrenches in common sizes.

replaceable roller-head types are available at most composite supply stores.

BRUSHES

Foam brushes work marginally well for very small projects, but will only work as long as the adhesive between the two foam halves in them holds up. Bristled brushes work best overall for dabbing resin into reinforcements, especially with large and curved-surface projects. Inexpensive brushes work well, but tug on the bristles beforehand to remove any loose bristles that may otherwise fall into the composite.

BLACK SHARPIE MARKER

These inexpensive black Sharpie markers are indispensable for marking patterns or cut-lines on fiberglass and aramid reinforcements. They are also helpful for marking trim lines on light-colored finished parts.

SILVER SHARPIE MARKER

Silver Sharpie markers apply a silver ink that has the appearance of fluid paint. They are very useful in marking pattern cut-lines on carbon fiber fabrics and final trim lines on dark-colored finished parts.

WHITE COLORED PENCIL

If you cannot find a silver Sharpie, a white or light colored pencil can work marginally well for drawing trim lines on dark colored parts.

GEL COAT GAUGE

A gel coat gauge is useful in determining the thickness of a wet gel coat. The gauge has several fingers on it which, when pressed against the gel coat, show how deep the gel coat is.

FIRE-RESISTANT TRASH RECEPTACLE

Solvent and chemical-soaked rags can pose a fire risk if they react or combust. To minimize this hazard, place all used rags in a fire-resistant trash container. If such a trash receptacle is not available, at the very least place rags in a metal trash can with a tight-fitting lid. Dispose of the rags daily, as required by local law, to avoid a dangerous build-up of reactive chemical waste.

Photo 8: Finishing work can be sped up considerably with a good jigsaw, sanders, and angle grinder.

SHELVING AND CABINETS

Organizing tools and materials is much easier with adequate shelving. Cabinets are additionally useful in locking up dangerous chemicals or tools from pets and children.

MOLD-MAKING TOOLS

Foam-shaping rasp

These inexpensive rasps can quickly remove material from a block of foam to rough out a desired form. They tend to work best with urethane foams, but can be used with styrene and Styrofoam even though they may tear out small pieces of foam when used. The cutting face on most rasps can be replaced once dull.

BUFFER (HANDHELD ELECTRIC)

An electric buffer can quickly polish large mold surfaces. Take care when using this tool — fast buffing creates friction and heat that can melt the release wax and smear it in the mold.

SAW (HAND SAW AND CARPENTER'S SAW)

Simple "old-school" hand-powered saws can quickly shape large soft materials, such as the foam or wood used in mold-making.

JIGSAW

For cutting curved shapes in flat material, an electric jigsaw works well. Use a blade that has teeth to match the thickness of the material to cut: fine-toothed blade for thin and hard materials, coarse-toothed blade for thick and soft materials.

BANDSAW

A bandsaw is especially helpful for cutting various thickness materials with better precision than a jigsaw. A bandsaw may not be necessary for your specific needs, but it can be helpful for some cutting tasks.

DRILL BITS

High-speed steel bits work well for drilling in sheet metal and wood. For drilling into composites, carbide or titanium-nitride bits will provide a much longer service life.

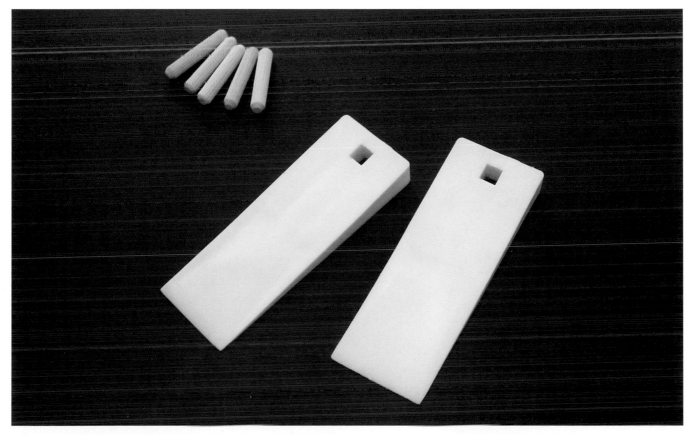

Photo 9: When demolding composite parts, wedges are indispensable. Dowels are excellent part ejection devices when designed correctly into a mold.

CORDLESS/CORDED DRILLS

A drill, whether corded, cordless, or on a drill press, is especially helpful for making mounting holes and other drilled features when building molds and finishing your composite parts.

ROUTER

For making roundovers, trimming rough edges, and making multiple copies of a part using a pattern, use a router with carbide bits.

SHEET METAL SNIPS

You may occasionally need to cut sheet metal to size for patterns or molds, so a set of good sheet metal snips in different sizes is helpful.

SCREWDRIVERS, CHISELS, AND SOCKET WRENCH SET

Procure a set of Phillips and standard screwdrivers in a few different sizes. Chisels come in handy for shaping and refining mold shapes in wood, plaster, and foam. A socket wrench is handy for tightening bolts on molds or inserted hardware.

HAMMERS

For applying some nice brute force, a few different hammers are helpful, such as ball-peen and claw hammers, along with a good rubber mallet.

PLIERS

Pliers in various sizes are good for anything from opening a seized resin canister to grasping the edge of a troublesome part during demolding.

Stainless steel ruler, flexible drafting tool, and shape gauge

Flexible metal rulers, like common stainless steel ones, are excellent for creating smooth curved guidelines for trimming or making patterns. A more expensive flexible drafting tool like the one shown are good for verifying the curvature of a part or for transferring a curve from one area of a part to another. Where a shape or contour needs to be copied from one area to another, a shape gauge can be additionally helpful.

VISE AND CLAMPS

A simple bench vise is great for securing your work as are c-clamps and wooden handscrews.

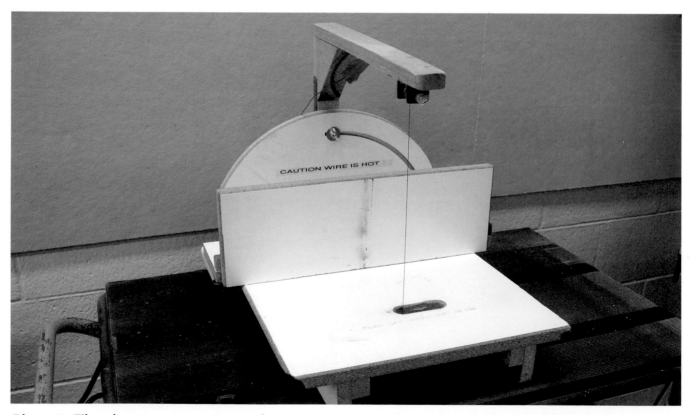

CAUTION WIRE IS HOT

Photo 10: Though not a necessary item, a hot wire cutter can make quick work of rough-shaping extruded or expanded styrene foams.

TABLESAW

For cutting large stock and ripping wood to size, a tablesaw can be indispensable. Always use a sharp blade and follow proper safety procedures when using a tablesaw. Though it will work, cutting composites on a tablesaw is not recommended without a carbide blade because of how abrasive composites can be to the blade's teeth.

DEMOLDING TOOLS

Plastic and metal putty knives

A putty knife can be useful for prying up the edges of a part in a mold to create spaces for wedges to be inserted. Use a hard plastic putty knife only on composite molds to avoid gouging the mold surfaces. Putty knives are also helpful for mixing fillers and spreading it on the surface of a composite.

PLASTIC WEDGES

Plastic wedges are pushed into thin spaces between the mold and part to help extract it from a mold. Never use any metal for this purpose as it will certainly damage the mold.

AIR COMPRESSOR AND AIR WEDGE

For some stubborn parts, air injected into gaps between the mold and part can loosen the part and push it out of the mold. Typical shop air compressor pressure (between 50 and 90 psi) is usually adequate and relatively safe.

WOODEN DOWELS/PEGS

If designed into a mold, wooden pegs can be very useful in pushing a part out of a mold, similar to how ejector pins push out a plastic part from an injection molding machine.

FINISHING TOOLS

Plastic tub or bin

When wet-sanding or using solvents in large quantities on a part, a plastic bin made of polypropylene or polyethylene is very helpful in minimizing any hazardous messes. Such tubs can be purchased at most housewares or home improvement stores, but make sure to get one large enough to fit big parts (such as a shallow one that is made to fit under a bed).

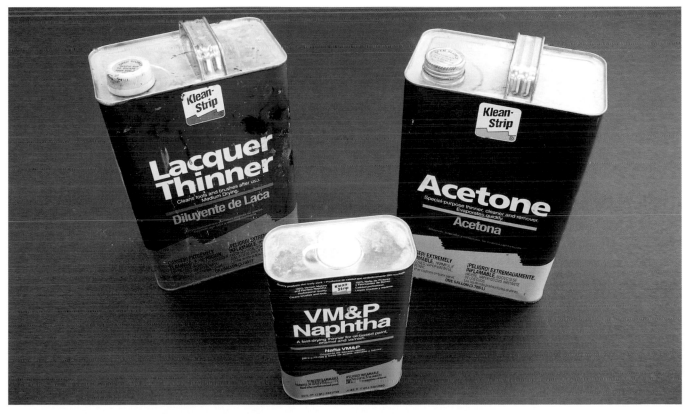

Photo 11: Have several solvents on hand for general clean-up tasks.

DREMEL/ROTARY TOOLS

Cut-off wheels and rotary files attached to a Dremel or rotary tool (either electric or air powered) can make quick work of trimming a composite part. The disposable abrasive nature of the cut-off wheel is excellent for straight, high quality cuts. Rotary files excel in creating curved or tight-radius cuts, especially when used in conjunction with a guide or template.

SANDING BLOCKS AND FILES

Because composites rarely come out of home-built molds without some imperfection in them, smoothing tools, such as sanding blocks and files, are indispensable. Anybody familiar with doing automotive bodywork will agree that the only way to ensure true surfaces is to use a sanding block. Likewise, a file can knock down edges and surfaces as needed for increased smoothness and quality.

ELECTRIC PALM SANDER AND BELT SANDER

Powered sanding of a composite with an electric palm sander (or an air powered dual action sander) or belt sander can significantly minimize the time and fatigue common with hand sanding. Some composites require considerable sanding, so these tools are definitely a wise investment. Air powered sanders have the added benefit of blowing sanding dust away from the work area.

ANGLE GRINDER

When working with thick, jagged-edged composites, a grinder can speedily remove material that would otherwise take considerable trimming time by hand filing or sanding. Always use fresh, high grit wheels to avoid overheating and burning the composite you are removing.

HACKSAW AND JIGSAW

Typical hacksaws and jigsaws are great for cutting laminates, but high quality carbide blades will last much longer than cheaper blades and require less overall cutting effort.

ADDITIONAL TOOLS

For most common home-built composites work, the above tools should suffice. However, several additional non-essential, or "wish-list", tools can be very helpful in a wet-layup composites shop. These tools include some of the following specialty items, all of which may be purchased from composites suppliers or other online or industrial sources.

HOT WIRE CUTTER

For cutting bulk shapes in styrene foams quickly and cleanly, not much beats a hot wire cutter. This high tension, electrically-heated wire melts through foam with ease and is commercially available in several sizes or can be built using simple online plans.

GEL COAT GUN

To apply smooth polyester gel coats, especially over large areas, a gel coat gun works wonders. They cost a bit and can take a little practice to use, but are worth their weight in gold once mastered.

ROLL STAND

If you plan on using multiple weights or types of reinforcement fabrics, a roll stand

Photo 12: Some composites will require filling and smoothing to develop quality cosmetic surfaces, so general auto body fillers will come to good use.

will provide immense help in organizing and moving your large, cumbersome rolls.

FIRE-PROOF CABINETS

Though these are listed as "non-essential", some local regulations (especially for businesses) require fire-proof cabinets for storing reactive chemicals in. For most home-built uses, they are not necessary, but certainly safer.

WHEELED TABLES OR SHELVES

Due to the variable sizes and shapes of many projects, the mobility offered by wheeled or movable tables and shelves can be very helpful. In fact, the utility of a small shop can be considerably enhanced if its tables and shelving can be reconfigured as needed.

DOWN-DRAFT SANDING TABLES

Composites mold-making and finishing often require laborious and dusty sanding. A down-draft sanding table can help to greatly minimize hazardous airborne dust by pulling it away from your workpiece.

WATER-JET CUTTER

Dust from composite parts can cause seveer wear on conventional cutting and machining equipment. Additionally, aramid fabrics do not cut well or cleanly without special tools. Though they can be expensive, if you have access to abrasive water-jet cutting equipment you will quickly find it useful for cleanly cutting all types of composites, especially if cutting them in large quantities.

LARGE OVEN

A mentioned, a resin's cure time will accelerate considerably if the composite is heated, and some epoxies or vinylester resins perform better once post-cured with heat. A common oven can work well to facilitate this, but be sure to follow the resin manufacturer's recommendations for maximum temperatures. Additionally, it is advisable to use a dedicated oven for this purpose rather than speeding up a cure in your kitchen oven — simply to avoid potential health risks.

HEAT BLANKETS

As with an oven, common heat blankets, like those used in cold climates for therapeutic purposes, can be placed in contact with a curing composite (separated by a thin polyethylene or nylon film) to speed its cure or provide post-curing.

MATERIALS AND CONSUMABLES
Solvents

Acetone and lacquer thinner work well for cleaning up resin spills and sticky tools. However, care should be taken when using these solvents near an uncured composite — if spilled on the composite, solvent can weaken it or keep it from curing completely.

Naphtha, a petroleum-based solvent available at most hardware stores, is useful in cleaning up modeling clay and oil residues. It will not attack a cured resin in the same way other solvents may.

Photo 13: To create a smooth, "Class-A" surface, nothing beats a good supply of sandpapers, a sanding block, files, and some good old elbow grease. A Dremel (or rotary tool) can quickly cut edges of a composite when used with a cut-off wheel or rotary file.

Screws, bolts, and nuts

A variety of common sizes made readily available in your shop can be beneficial in various mold-making procedures.

Body filler

Body filler is used for filling imperfections and small gaps in a plug or mold. General body fillers are adequate for most mold-making uses.

Wall compound

For quick, inexpensive build up on a plug or mold, wall compound can be purchased in large buckets and is more cost effective than body filler. However, it is much softer than body filler, and can be sanded through very quickly.

Sandpaper

For shaping and smoothing the materials used in composites fabrication, some basic sandpaper, ranging in grits from 80 to 220, are important.

Wet-sandpaper (up to fine grits)

A variety of wet-sandpapers from 240 to 2000 grits are used for achieving a high-quality surface finish on parts and molds. For fast material removal, some wet-sandpapers are available as course as 80 grit — a very useful alternative to the dust produced by dry, heavy grit sandpapers.

Rubbing compound

Rubbing compound is a thick liquid or paste that contains very fine grains for polishing out the scratches left in a mold surface by sandpaper. Different abrasive strengths are available, depending on the final surface shine you desire for your mold.

Cloths

Terry cloths are helpful in wiping up general chemical spills. These cloths are also effective in buffing wax mold-release.

Soft cotton cloths are good for applying mold-release paste wax and PVA.

General soft-paper cleanup rags are an inexpensive aid for keeping hands and tools clean during a layup.

Mold-release/parting wax (paste wax)

When it comes to mold-release wax (also known as "parting wax"), it is good to get a high-quality wax rather than to take a chance with a low-cost substitute (such as car wax) — effortlessly removing your part from a mold depends on it!

PVA liquid

Polyvinyl-alcohol (PVA) is a liquid mold-release available from composites distributors that is applied and dried over mold-release wax. It acts as a water-soluble second line of defense against parts sticking to a mold. It can be brushed or wiped onto a waxed mold, but is best applied with a small hobby airbrush or refillable aerosol spray can, available at hobby or hardware stores.

Heat shrink tape

This is a special non-adhesive clear heat shrink tape that contracts in length when heated. It is wound around a mandrel-formed composite and heated to provide fiber-consolidating pressure.

Heat shrink tubing

Similar to heat shrink tape — but in a tube form — heat shrink tubing can be used for mandrel-formed layups, though

Photo 14: For wiping on waxes and mold releases, or for simply cleaning up spills and debris, have a variety of rags and towels ready.

it is available in limited diameter sizes and must have a special release on it for use with composites. This specialty item can be difficult to find (see the Additional Readings and Resources section for more information).

MASKING TAPE

Common painter's masking tape is great for keeping resin off certain areas of a mold or workspace and for otherwise protecting surfaces from scratches.

POLYETHYLENE FLASH TAPE

Polyethylene flash tape is used to provide a stretchy, removable mold-release in selected areas. It can be a bit expensive when purchased from composites suppliers, but works very well.

PACKING TAPE

Clear packing tape can be very useful in masking off an area that needs additional release from resins, and is a very effective (though less stretchy) substitute for flash tape. Most resins will not adhere to packing tape, and just chip off once cured

SEALANT TAPE

Sealant tape is a gummy, sticky silicone-based tape that comes on rolls with removable backing from composites suppliers. It is used primarily for vacuum-bagging techniques, but is still handy for use in other layup procedures.

MASTIC TAPE

An inexpensive replacement for sealant tape, this common construction tape cannot be stretched to pull out wrinkles in the way sealant tape can, but can still be effective for many fabrication uses.

EXTRUDED OR EXPANDED STYRENE FOAM

These foams are used in construction for insulating homes, and are readily available at most home improvement stores in large sheets.

They cut very easily with a utility knife or handsaw and shape quickly with a rasp. Because of their relatively low cost and ease of use, they are great for making large, bulky forms. Polyester and vinylester resins will dissolve styrene foam if it has not first been sealed, but it can be used in direct contact with epoxy resins without any problem. Using a rasp on expanded styrene (such as Styrofoam) tends to "blow out" small pieces of the foam, whereas the extruded styrene shapes much more smoothly.

URETHANE FOAM OR VINYL FOAM

Urethane and vinyl foams are very stable with all resin systems. They come in a variety of densities, measured in terms of their weight per cubic foot. For example, "10lb foam" is a medium-density foam that weighs about ten pounds per cubic foot. These foams are excellent for building large plugs and molds — though they can be a bit expensive — and are easily cut with a handsaw and formed with a rasp.

TWO-PART URETHANE FOAM

For filling odd shapes and large gaps, two-part urethane foams are available from several sources. They come in various densities and are formed by

Photo 15: Use high quality parting waxes and mold releases formulated specifically for composites molding. Also have a supply of brushes for general layup use, along with rubbing compound for taking scratches out of mold surfaces.

simply mixing measured volumes of each part together. The two chemical components react with each other, and foam up to fill whatever volume they are poured into. The reaction time of these foams depends on the temperature, but will start foaming very quickly once they are mixed. It is not advisable to use the inexpensive urethane foam insulation available in spray cans from hardware stores; some of these foams can become soft again when coated or removed from contact with air.

FLAT OR FORMABLE SHEET MATERIALS

Plastic sheets ranging from 1/16" to 1/4" thick are easily formable with a heat gut or oven (as demonstrated in chapter six), have very smooth surfaces, and are excellent for producing quick, simple geometric molds.

Sheet wood, such as melamine, masonite, and medium-density fiberboard (MDF) can make good jigs, mold supports, and other reinforce-ments, but porous woods should be sealed prior to using them as a mold surface.

Sheet metal can be formed into durable molds with complex shapes using typical metalworking tools. It can also be polished to a high-quality mir-ror finish and is great for forming high-volume production composite parts.

PLASTIC FILM (3-5MIL THICK)

Polyethylene plastic film (3-5mils thick) is excellent for protecting tabletops and other sur-faces from resin spills. These films also work well for separating workspaces or for covering an uncured layup to protect it from dust and debris.

ABSORBENT SAND

One good way to clean up a large resin spill is to spread absorbent sand, sawdust, wood chips or cat litter over the mess. Allow it to absorb for while, then use a shop broom or shovel to scoop it up. Dispose of the spilled material as local safety

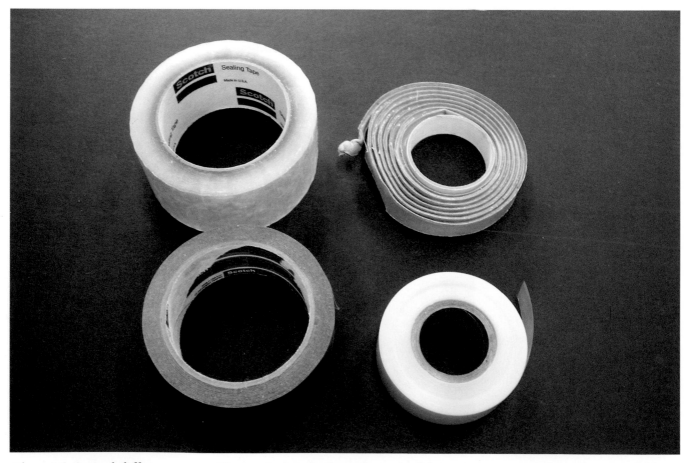

Photo 16: Several different tapes will come in handy throughout the fabrication process, so keep these available for quick use.

regulations require.

GLOVES (NITRILE OR LATEX RUBBER)

Thin latex rubber, nitrile, or vinyl gloves are important in keeping resins and solvents from coming in contact with your skin. Find a reliable pair of disposable gloves (usually available in boxes of multiple pairs) that are not too tight and not too loose. Tight gloves can cause hand cramps, while loose gloves can slip off or cause general frustration during a layup.

MODELING CLAY

Non-hardening oil-based modeling clay, available from art stores and some composites distributors, works well for creating temporary fillets and for filling gaps or imperfections in molds and plugs.

RELEASE PLY FABRIC

This fabric is usually used in more advanced molding techniques that utilize vacuum-bagging equipment, yet it is very useful in producing secondarily-bondable surfaces on a composite. Simply place a piece of this porous, self-releasing fabric anywhere on the surface of your uncured composite where you intend to later bond on additional materials, hardware, or additional composite parts.

CHAPTER CONCLUSION

Though the list of space, tools, and materials requirements for fabricating composites can be a bit long, many of the needed items already exist in most garages and shops. Other necessary items are readily available from local and online hardware and composites supply stores, some of which are listed in the Additional Resources section. Once these basic tools have been acquired, you are ready to begin composites fabrication.

Photo 17: Depending on the application, one mold-building material or another may be appropriate. Shown (from the bottom) are acrylic plastic sheet, sheet metal, melamine-faced particle board, and modeling clay.

Chapter Five

Composites Molding Basics

Performing a Basic Wet-layup

There are several different wet layup methods that can be employed to fabricate composites although they all follow the same basic steps. Whatever the method, however, the mold used in the lamination process should be prepared with high-quality release agents and all lamination materials organized prior to even mixing the resin

for the layup. The simplest lamination steps and procedures can be found in the building of a flat panel composite.

STAGES OF COMPOSITES FABRICATION

There are six basic stages that any composite will pass through before completion. They are common to any lamination process, even if the

Photo 3: Calipers can be used to measure a fabric's thickness if it is unknown.

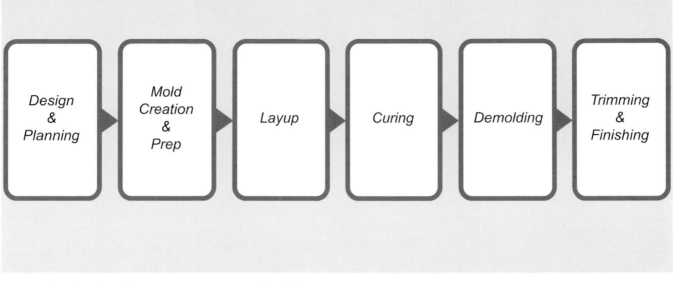

Illustration 1: The six stages common to wet-layup fabrication methods.

particular details of one process are considerably different from another. These stages are shown in illustration 1. Though they may seem like a long list of steps, they will become second nature as you become familiar with working in composites.

DESIGN & PLANNING

One of the greatest skills you can develop in working with composites will be your ability to competently design and plan the composite project from start to finish. To do this, you will need to finalize the shape, and then adequately prepare all the needed materials for a smooth layup and part finish. Any number of mishaps can happen during the course of a composite project, but the situations that are probably the most aggravating arise from one of two things: a poorly devised molding system, or not being

Sample Flat Panel Lamination Schedule

Resin System: Epoxy

Surface Coat (thickened epoxy with pigment)

2 Layers - 6 oz. fiberglass, plain weave
(fibers parallel to mold edges)

4 Layers - 10 oz. fiberglass, plain weave
(fibers parallel to mold edges)

Illustration 2: Lamination schedule for the layup of a simple demonstration panel.

Photo 4: A ruler and Sharpie marker help in laying out the size and shape of the reinforcements you will use in a layup.

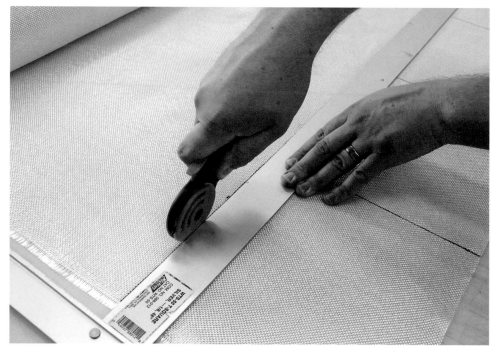

Photo 5: For cutting thin fabrics, a rotary cutter (available at fabric stores) will cut cleanly and with little hassle.

completely prepared to finish a layup once you've started. These situations are exactly what the design and planning stage is meant to help avoid.

MOLD CREATION & PREP

Unlike many metal parts, composites simply cannot be created without some shape about which they can be formed. Creating the mold and properly preparing it can take a significant amount of time but will make or break the success of your parts. A well-built mold is worth its weight in gold, but it must also be prepared before each use to ensure good removal (or "release") of the finished parts so it can be used again. Even so-called "moldless" composites (which we will explore later) require sufficient preparation for a high quality composite to be formed on them.

Any preparation for layup should include gathering together all those tools and materials you intend to use during the layup. This will include mixing and measuring equipment, scissors, spreaders and brushes, gloves, protective table coverings, wax and PVA release, resins, and reinforcements.

LAYUP

In the "layup" stage, the fabricator joins the resin and reinforcement together in the mold to form the composite. This step is where the "rubber meets the road" — where all your molding preparations come

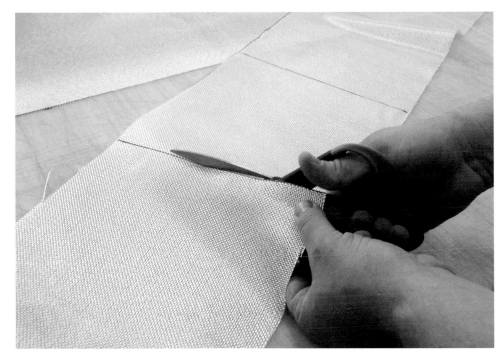

composite before progressing to the next step. The curing of resins can be accelerated using heat lamps, heating pads, or an oven on low heat. For some epoxies, it is even suggested to "post-cure" the resin prior to use by raising the temperature of the composite for better curing — something that is most easily achieved by placing it in a large oven at the recommended temperature. As a precaution, if you intend to use heat for curing, make

Photo 6: Thick or aramid-based fabrics are best cut with a pair of high-quality scissors.

together in a gooey manifestation of composite creation. It is probably the messiest of the steps, and can at times be a bit frustrating if the resin-soaked fabric pieces do not quite fit or lay down as well as you would like. However this is by far the most hands-on of the composites steps. If you love to get your hands dirty, this will likely be your "happy place".

CURING

After completing a layup, a fabricator will step back and allow the composite to cure. For any fabricator that is molding a new part for the first time, this can entail a great deal of relief once the layup has been successfully completed, but also a sense of hope that the final part will come with all the perfection you've planned into it. If you happened to be one of those kids who always got too curious about your Christmas gifts, avoid getting antsy or fidgety with the mold and uncured laminate at this stage — disturbing the composite during cure can severely compromise its quality. Allow sufficient time for cure, closely following the resin manufacturer's recommendations for good solid and complete cross-linking of the resin in the

Photo 7: Loosely woven fabrics may fray and leave messy fibers in a layup. Pulling out a couple yarns near each edge can help minimize this.

Photo 8: Stack your fabric in the order you will be using it in a layup—with the first layer on top.

Photo 9: A simple non-porous surface, such as a melamine-faced board, makes a good mold for a flat panel.

sure your heat sources does not overheat the resin as this may weaken the composite or deform the part.

DEMOLDING

Removing your cured part from a mold, also known as the "demolding" step, can be the most exciting, and yet nerve-racking, of these six stages. On the one hand, anticipation builds to see the final results of the molded part for the first time after it has been cured and removed from the mold. On the other hand, it can be stressful removing a stubborn part while trying to avoid damaging the mold. Further, if the part does not come out as planned, (i.e., with a bad surface finish, poor lamination or large voids), it can mean that the part may have to be laboriously reconstructed again. Demolding can be improved by adequately arranging for it in the Design & Planning stage.

TRIMMING & FINISHING

In order to have a truly polished part that you will be proud to display, the trimming and finishing stage cannot be understated. Nearly all composites require trimming after demolding to remove flashing, clean up edges, or add holes and cuts required for the final part. Likewise, composites very rarely come out of a mold without the need for some surface finishing, especially without the use of advanced processes (such as mass-production compression molding or autoclaving).

Whenever discussing molding techniques for composites, the very common chicken-and-egg question always arises: "How do I create composites if I don't have a mold in the first place?" The advice I always give to beginners is to start practicing composites building techniques by creating simple panels using flat, hard, and non-porous surfaces — like melamine, plastic sheet, or thick sheet metal — as a mold. A panel may not have the curvaceous interest of a more complex part, but it will help you get your hands into the molding process without making costly initial errors. This chapter will cover some of the basics of preparing molds along with a few common molding processes that can be done without complex or expensive molds.

PLANNING FOR MOLDING

Once you have decided on a molding process, completed your mold, and have reviewed chapter two on Matrices and Reinforcements to choose a good resin and reinforcement system, you will be well on your way to getting started. Next, you will need to determine the "lamination schedule" for your composite (see illustration 2). This refers to the number of layers, the types of fabric, their order of layering, and their orientation in the mold during layup. Resolving these matters prior to starting the actual composite layup will help to

Photo 10: Clean your mold surface completely with warm water or solvent (as appropriate) before use. Foreign matter may adversely affect the composite.

Photo 11: Porous edges can be sealed to easily release from cured resin by covering them with packing tape.

57

Photo 12: Cover edges all around to keep resin from bonding to them.

avoid confusion and minimize layup time.

The fiber type and weave, weight, orientation, and number of layers will be driven by your particular composite application, and can be further determined by your own analysis and experience. Remember that lightweight fabrics are good for thin laminates and smooth surfaces, while heavy fabrics are best for quick laminate build-up. To get a good "ballpark" thickness for your planned composite, layup some small strips of your desired composite material in different thicknesses (as outlined in the flat panel lamination steps below) to see how they perform. If you have a sample (such as with an existing composite part that you would like to reproduce) and you need to find the number of layers in it, measure the thickness of the fabric you intend to use with a dial or digital caliper, then divide the sample's thickness by the thickness of your fabric — this should get you relatively close (see photo 3). Simple flat samples can be very helpful in visualizing and testing the strength potential of a composite panel. However, compound curved surfaces are always more rigid than flat ones, so it may be possible to laminate less plies into a composite part that has any amount of contour and shape to it. As you test out these thicknesses, keep track of (and write down) the materials and number of

Photo 13: A rounded stick or spreader can smooth modeling clay into tight corners or seams in a mold.

layers you intend for your final part and include them in the lamination schedule. Note any changes to your lamination schedule that may occur during testing and production of your parts, as they will make future layups with your mold much easier.

After determining your lamination schedule, cut the fabric into the size and shape necessary to fit the mold. A piece of scrap fabric (in the same weave as the fabric you will be using) can work well as a pattern if you are cutting several pieces of the same shape. Make sure to cut your fabric slightly larger than its intended finished dimensions — an inch or two extra on each side should be sufficient for most parts (see photos 4 - 6). This excess will ensure that you have enough material to cover your mold surfaces. As some fabrics tend to fray and drop stray fibers into a layup when

handled, manually pull out the first couple of yarns at the edges of each fabric piece to keep them from falling out on their own (see photo 7). This will save considerable hassle once the layup has begun. Stack these reinforcement layers on a table in the opposite order they will be laid into the mold: the first layers to go in the mold should be on the top of the fabric stack (see photo 8).

PREPARING A MOLD FOR LAYUP

Correctly preparing the mold can prevent a multitude of potential problems. If the mold surface is not sufficiently smooth, cleaned and waxed, parts may seize to the mold, rendering the part unusable. Even worse, the mold may end up being damaged or destroyed — wasting the time and

Photo 15: Apply wax in thin (yet complete) coats.

Photo 14: Always use a high-quality wax made specifically for composite layups.

Photo 16: Once the wax has dried, buff off any haze to reveal a smooth, shiny mold surface, and then apply the next coat of wax.

Photo 18: Spraying is the preferred method for applying PVA, especially if multiple coats are required.

Photo 19: PVA can also be applied by pouring it directly on or into a mold...

Photo 20: ...and then wiped onto the mold surface completely and uniformly before it becomes tacky or dry.

Photo 17: Refillable aerosol sprayers can be filled with polyvinyl alcohol (PVA) for ease of application.

materials invested in the mold's creation. To minimize problems, follow these simple steps, shown on a simple melamine board (measuring 12" square by ?" thick) that will be used later for our practice panel lamination layup (see photo 9).

First, completely clean the mold surface with a cloth and warm water, and then wipe it dry with another clean cloth (see photo 10). If local cleaning of any stubborn foreign material is needed, carefully scrape it from the surface or apply appropriate solvents, such as lacquer thinner and acetone (for uncured resin), or naphtha (for oil or clay) in sparing amounts to completely clean the surface.

In the case of molds that have porous areas (such as with the edges of the melamine board we will use for the panel lamination), it is best to protect those surfaces with something that will allow it to release from the cured resin. Flash tape or clear packing tape work well for this as they have a natural release that prevents bonding to the resin (see photos 11 and photo 12).

If you are working with a mold that has seams — as is the case with multi-part molds — or if your mold has unnecessarily sharp, inner corners or tight features modeling clay can be used to fill such gaps by using your finger or a rounded stick end to create a filleted corner. Cleanly bridging such areas will make it easier to layup the laminate over the seams or into the corners (see photo 13).

Use a high-quality wax, such as a paste or brush-on wax developed specifically for use with polyester and epoxy resin systems (see photo 14). Follow any special instructions listed on the wax's packaging. With a paste wax, rub the wax on with a cloth, and then allow the wax to dry away from direct sunlight or heat sources (see photo 15). Avoid applying too much wax; complete coverage with a thin film of wax should suffice for each wax layer. Buff off the wax film with a soft cloth until you can see the shine of the smooth mold surface, and then add repeated wax layers as needed (see photo 16). A new mold will require a minimum of four wax applications. "Seasoned" (or well-used) molds may require two or less wax treatments.

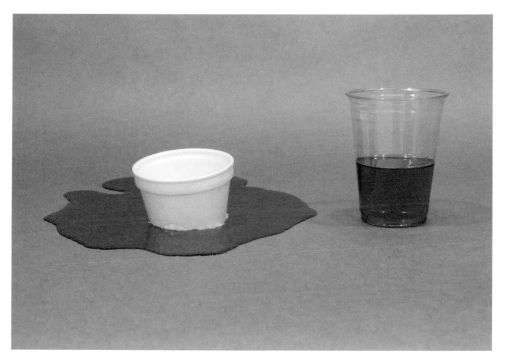

Photo 21: Polyester or vinylester resins will eventually dissolve any mixing cup that is made of styrene. Common mixing containers suitable with these resins include those made from polyethylene (HDPE or LDPE), polypropylene (PP), or un-waxed paper tubs.

Photo 22: Always mix resin thoroughly! Scrape the sides and bottom of the mixing container to mix all the resin and hardener/catalyst together.

Photo 23: *If adding pigment to your resin, use a separate mixing stick to mix up the pigment particles before use as they will tend to sink to the bottom of the container over time.*

When applying wax to areas with clay on them, be careful to rub the wax lightly over the clay surface. Avoid picking up any of the clay with the cloth as it can easily spread onto the waxed surface.

Apply the polyvinyl alcohol (PVA) onto the mold surface to create a full-coverage thin film. A PVA film creates a water soluble barrier that further prevents resins from adhering to a mold surface. PVA is best applied with a spray gun in multiple coats, allowing it to dry completely between coats (see photo 17 and photo 18). It will be evident that the PVA has dried completely when it has lost its surface sheen. PVA can also be applied by generously wiping it onto the mold surface with a rag, but will likely produce faint wipe lines in the final laminate's surface due to any uneven application (see photos 19 and 20). PVA release films can be fragile and will tear easily, so use care and avoid touching the surface after it has dried.

Shield the mold from any dust or foreign matter (including curious fingers) that may otherwise damage the prepared mold surface. Use a painter's drop cloth, such as an inexpensive polyethylene drop cloth, to protect the mold until all the materials for layup are ready.

Photo 24: *When adding pigment to a resin, scrape it onto the side of the resin mixing container and then mix it into the resin with your mixing stick. This will avoid any contamination of resin into the pigment.*

BASIC PANEL LAMINATION USING A GEL/SURFACE COAT

Now that the mold is ready for layup, you can now begin to prepare a special surface protection, called a "gel coat" or "surface coat". Some composites may experience environments that can cause excessive abrasion or where high humidity may produce fabric print-through. A composite may also require special coloring or surface effects. For these applications, a coating of resin is generally applied to the mold prior to the composite being laid over it. Such surface treatments are common in boats and hot tubs, but are also beneficial anywhere a durable surface is needed and the composite's weight is not critical. These coatings generally add excess weight, and can be relatively brittle, yet are sought after when their advantages outweigh their disadvantages. The term "gel coat" generally refers to special-purpose, gelled polyester resin coat, whereas a thickened epoxy resin coat is called a "surface coat". Gel and surface coatings provide the best service when they actually cross-link with the composite laminate they are protecting. In this way they differ from a "flood coat" that is applied onto an already fully-cured composite (which will be discussed in the Finishing Techniques chapter).

Photo 25: As with mixing the resin itself, mix pigment into the resin as thoroughly as possible.

Photo 26: If your resin is not mixed completely (or your mixing ratios are wrong) the resin may not cure correctly — or at all, as shown here.

Photo 27: Scoop filler in small amounts. A little goes a long way.

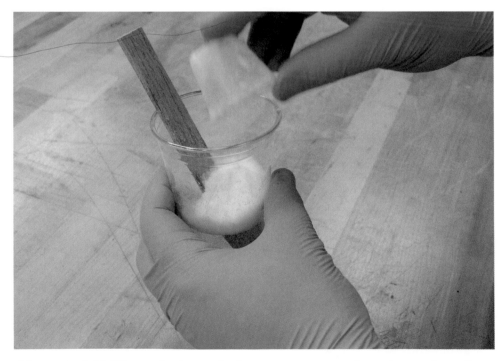

Photo 28: Add filler and mix it a little at a time to avoid creating pockets of filler in the resin.

The following directions include several general guidelines for mixing and using gel/surface coats. However, you should always read the instructions provided by your particular resin's manufacturer. Whenever using polyester, vinylester, or polyester gel coat resins, make sure to mix them in a polyethylene, polypropylene, or un-waxed paper cup so the resin won't dissolve the sides of the container; the styrene monomer in polyester and vinylester resins will attack any styrene based plastic and dissolve it (see photo 21). When mixing, always make sure to scrape the sides and bottom of the mixing container as much as possible during mixing so the resin and catalyst/hardener will be completely combined (see photo 22).

Polyester gel coats come clear or in a variety of pigmented colors. They will accept fillers, such as glitter or special effect flakes, and can be easily color-matched with an existing paint color. Before adding pigments of your own to a gel coat, be sure to thoroughly mix the pigment in its container; pigment particles tend to settle to the bottom of the container over time (see photo 23). Use a clean stick to add pigment to the gel coat mixture — in amounts recommended by the pigment manufacturer — by dipping it into the pigment container, then scraping the pigment from the stick onto the interior rim of the gel coat mixing container so it can be easily stirred in by the mixing stick (see photos 24 and 25).

If a color blend is required (such as in creating a special purple through the mixing of a blue and a red pigment), slowly add the pigments to the gel coat using separate sticks until the desired color is obtained. Be careful not to accidentally cross-contaminate pigment colors by inadvertently inserting a pigment-coated stick from one color container into

Photo 29: Again, mix filler into the resin completely.

another. Likewise, avoid getting any gel coat resin in the pigment container. If adding glitter flake (or other additive), again, make sure that it is fully mixed before application.

If using a spray gun that requires pre-mixing of the gel coat before spraying, catalyze the gel coat with MEKP as directed by the manufacturer. Conversely, if using a spray gun that mixes the gel coat as it is being sprayed, follow the instructions specific to the gun, adjusting for proper catalyst mixture in the spray.

When an epoxy resin system is required for your composite, epoxy surface coats are available from some manufacturers. However, if you need to create your own surface coat, it is not difficult to do. Resin thickeners are available for this specific purpose, and each should be mixed with the resin and tested on vertical surfaces (checking to see if it will run down the

Photo 30: Use long, smooth strokes when applying gel or surface coats with a brush.

Photo 31: A proper surface coat should be self-leveling but not slough off the mold surfaces.

Photo 32: To check if a gel or surface coat is ready for reinforcements to be laid-up over it, touch it lightly with a gloved finger: if resin comes off on the glove, it is not ready for layup yet.

surface) to determine proper viscosity prior to actual application in the mold. It is not recommended to apply a thickened epoxy surface coat with a spray gun, as its consistency may clog up the gun or otherwise prove problematic while spraying.

To thicken an epoxy resin for use in a surface coat, first choose one that will allow enough pot life for the mixing in of thickeners — typically 30 minutes or more should be sufficient unless you need more time to cover a large surface. Measure out the correct ratios of hardener and resin and then mix the resin and hardener as completely as possible; failing to mix the resin sufficiently may leave soft spots of poorly cured resin in the surface coat (see photo 26). Slowly add an appropriate thickening agent, such as colloidal silica, to the resin mixture, stirring it as thoroughly as possible to minimize any clumping of the thickener in the resin (see photos 27 - 29). Add only enough thickener to bring the epoxy mixture to the viscosity of molasses (not peanut butter) — it should still be mostly self-leveling and leave minimal brush strokes once applied to a surface. You can then add pigment or other cosmetic additives to the thickened epoxy mixture in the same way as explained for polyester gel coats. When the consistency is correct and mixed with pigment, apply the surface coat to the mold faces until they are sufficiently covered (see photos 30 and 31).

Though this particular panel layup calls for brush application of the gel/surface coat, it is generally not recommended to use a brush because it is difficult to maintain a uniform, streak-free coating. However, for small projects — especially those involving mostly flat, horizontal surfaces — or when using a thickened epoxy-based system, an inexpensive chip brush can save considerable preparation and clean-up time if care is taken to ensure that no brush strokes are left in the gel coat prior to lamination of the reinforcement. Because of how much effort and chemical cleaning it takes to make a brush reusable after using it to apply a gel/surface coat, it is usually advisable to allow the resin on it to cure and then simply discard it.

If using a brush to apply the gel/surface coat, spread it on in a couple thick layers, rather than in many thin layers, as you would with paint. Thicker layers offer better self-support when brushed on in addition to creating less cleanup hassle between coats. If applying polyester gel coat as a spray, do so in thin layers opting for using a spray gun made specifically for applying gel coats. A gel coat thickness gauge (available from resin suppliers) is helpful in monitoring the thickness of your gel/surface coat. Simply press the edge of the gauge onto the

Photo 33: A gel coat that is ready for layup will leave little or no resin on a gloved finger, but will still leave a slight mark on its surface where the glove touched it.

Photo 34: Pour resin over the surface of the gel coat to help wet the fabric from beneath.

Photo 35: Smooth out the resin so it will soak into the fabric more uniformly.

uncured gel/surface coat; the highest gauge finger to have resin on it will indicate the gel/surface coat thickness. A thickness of 20 to 25 mils (.020" to .025") is common for a single polyester gel coat, but thickened epoxy surface coats can be even thicker (especially for molds) — up to 1/8" thick or more. The gel/surface coat can be built up in several layers to be as thick as needed — but remember that thicker coatings are generally more brittle and may chip or crack very easily. With good planning, different colors of gel coat may even be applied to masked surfaces for interesting aesthetic/graphic effects.

In order to promote good polymer cross-linking and bonding between layers, each successive gel/surface coat layer should be applied while the previous layer is still tacky. This tacky state can be readily determined by touching a discrete section of the gel/surface coat with a gloved finger. If resin sticks to your finger, it is not quite ready; but if your finger leaves a sticky impression on the surface without picking up any resin, the coat is ready for subsequent layers (see photos 32 and 33).

Mix the resin for the layup as directed by the resin manufacturer and begin the layup while the gel/surface coat is still tacky. Pour some resin into the mold and then use a squeegee or brush to level the resin over the tacky

Photo 36: Carefully place the first layer of fabric over the wet resin and gel/surface coat. Avoid introducing any large wrinkles into the fabric as they may be difficult to remove.

gel/surface coated faces of the mold (see photos 34 and 35). This initial coating of resin will allow better wet-out of the first fabric layer from beneath while also holding it in place. Carefully place the first layer of reinforcement fabric into the mold, avoiding any tugging of the fabric that may warp the weave (see photos 36 and 37). Apply light, sweeping pressure on the fabric with the squeegee or brush to help work the resin through the fiber (see photo 38). If resin from below does not fully wet out the fabric, add more resin to the top and brush or squeeze it in until the fibers are fully wet (see photo 39). Fiberglass will go from opaque to transparent as the resin saturates it, whereas aramid fabrics will become deeper in color once saturated. It is difficult to see when carbon fiber is fully wetted out because of its matte black color, but it will begin to show a slight surface sheen when saturated (see photo 40). Next, begin applying the additional fabric layers one at a time, as designated by the lamination schedule (see photo 41). Continue to add resin to the top of the layers and work it through with the squeegee/brush (or even with your fingers) as needed for full resin saturation. Work out any bubbles or excess resin from the laminate as they will weaken it. Bubbles can cause voids from which cracks and delamination can originate, while too much resin simply

Photo 37: Use your fingers or a spreader to carefully flatten the fabric against the resin surface. Lightly work out any bubbles or wrinkles.

Photo 38: Use the spreader to even out any dry spots in the fabric.

Photo 39: Add more resin on top of the fabric layer to prepare it for the next ply of fabric.

adds weight (and brittleness) without adding any significant strength. Continue applying more layers and resin until the entire laminate is complete, as determined by the lamination schedule.

Once the layup is complete, the laminate should be allowed to cure sufficiently before demolding (see photo 42). The length of time required for full cure of the lamination depends on the particular resin system, the thickness of the laminate, the presence of UV or infrared light, ambient temperature, and the temperature of the mold. While many common resins will cure to a gel state at room temperature within a couple hours, manufacturers often recommend leaving the laminate in the mold for at least twelve to twenty-four hours (or more) to allow it to fully harden. Some resins may even require a post-cure cycle in which additional temperature is applied. Be sure to follow the manufacturer's recommended instructions for your type of resin. For information on removing your part from a mold see the chapter on Demolding Techniques.

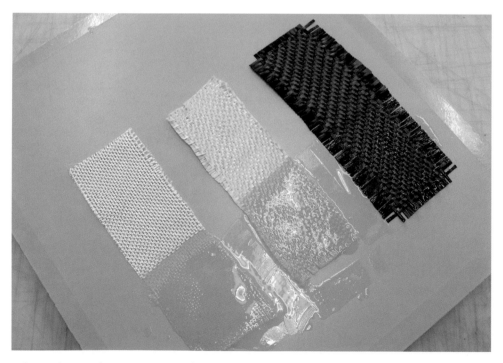

Photo 40: Make sure to entirely wet-out the fabric. Once wet, fiberglass will become translucent, aramids will gain deeper color, and carbon will increase in its surface sheen, as shown by these examples.

CHAPTER CONCLUSION

The steps of composite fabrication are distinct and of specific importance to the entire process of creating a composite. Adhering to a plan for building the composite and then following through on all the necessary mold preparation steps will help ensure a high quality composite part. In fact, simple, non-porous sheet materials, common resins, and inexpensive reinforcements can produce a very basic yet functional flat panel composite.

Photo 41: Add additional layers of fabric one at a time, wetting them with additional resin, as needed until the lamination schedule is complete.

Photo 42: Here is the finished panel layup ready for curing, demolding, and trimming.

Chapter Six

Composites Fabrication Techniques

Three Simple Lamination Methods

A myriad of fabrication techniques are available to composites builders. Some are very specialized and of limited application while others are commonly used to build a wide range of composites. Three techniques that are useful to the average fabricator include "rigidized acrylic" lamination, mandrel lamination, and "moldless" lamination.

The continual development of advanced composite technologies over the past sixty years has lead to a wide range of fabricating methods that meet the varied needs of building different composite structures. Many of these fabrication processes have been alluded to already, but there are a few techniques that have proven to be particularly useful to homebuilders. Among these are techniques for building composites that require minimal tooling or molds and can be performed with-

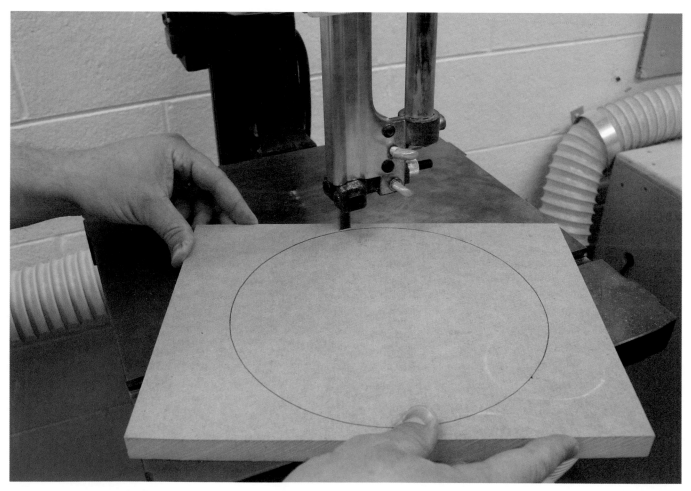

Photo 2: Cut a circle form out of MDF to mold the acrylic. The circle should be slightly larger than the actual speaker.

out expensive equipment, even in the most humble of workshops or garages. One of these methods includes heat forming plastic sheet and reinforcing it with composite materials. Another method allows the fabricator to build straight tubing using woven sock, while yet another allows the composite to be laid over a foam structure that has been carved to shape using simple tools.

"RIGIDIZED ACRYLIC" LAMINATION METHOD

One way of forming composites without complex or expensive molds is by using a method called "rigidized acrylic" lamination. This type of lamination is employed by manufacturers of bathtubs and some small boats because it produces durable parts with very smooth outer surfaces. To create these laminates, a thin sheet of colored, opaque acrylic plastic (also known by the trade names "Plexiglas" and "Lucite") is heated and vacuum-thermoformed over a mold, and then allowed to cool into shape. After this thermoforming step, a reinforcement fiber is laminated onto the backside of the resulting plastic shell using a polyester or vinylester resin. In this way, the plastic shell acts as both a mold and an integral part of the final composite.

In large production facilities, vacuum-thermoforming equipment can quickly shape parts with relative ease. However, in a small shop or home-built environment, an oven, heat gun, and simple wooden forms can be equally effective at shaping the acrylic. In fact, outside of rigidized acrylic composites, heating and forming acrylic plastic sheet can be a fast, effective, and low cost way to create actual limited-use molds for some composites. Acrylic sheet requires a little practice, though, to understand how to form it best. If you have never used this material before, cut some strips of acrylic on a table saw or band saw and then heat

---

Speaker Panel Rigidized Acrylic Lamination Schedule

Resin System: Vinylester

Acrylic Form (from sheet stock)

10 Layers - 10 oz. fiberglass mat

Illustration 1: Lamination schedule for the layup of a rigidized acrylic speaker panel.

Photo 3: Sand down any irregular surfaces around the form using a belt-sander, and then using a router to round over the edge. Sand all edges smooth.

Photo 4: Build a wood frame the same size as the acrylic.

Photo 5: Drill clearance holes for screws into the top frame and through the acrylic.

Photo 6: Prepare the acrylic for thermoforming by removing its backing paper or film.

Photo 7: Use screws to tighten the acrylic into the frame.

Photo 8: Place the frame and acrylic into an oven at about 375 degrees Fahrenheit for a few minutes.

Photo 9: Check the acrylic periodically (every minute or so) to see how soft it is.

Photo 10: When the acrylic begins to sag, it will be close to being workable. It will be ready when it has the feel of floppy wet leather.

Photo 11: Once ready, remove the acrylic from the oven…

Photo 12: …and quickly clamp it to a table to make it more manageable.

Photo 13: Hold the form in your hand…

Photo 14: …and press it into the acrylic to form the speaker mounting surface.

Photo 15: Pressure from a leather-gloved hand can help shape the hot plastic, if necessary. Be careful not to scratch it.

Photo 16: Once the plastic has cooled, remove it from the frame and wipe off any dust or debris that may be left over.

Photo 19: Thoroughly wipe and clean the surface that the layup will bond to.

Photo 17: Use masking tape to apply a protective plastic cover over the front face of the acrylic to minimize the possibility of scratching the surface.

Photo 21: Lay in the first ply of fiberglass mat, dabbing resin into it with a brush while adding resin as needed to completely saturate it.

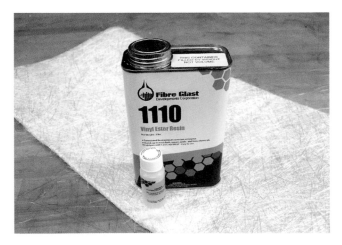

Photo 18: Vinylester and fiberglass mat are a good combination for this layup application. Prepare all the pieces of fiberglass mat necessary for layup.

Photo 22: Place additional mat strips into the form, overlapping them onto the previous layer. Wet these out with resin until there is good coverage all around.

Photo 23: Add larger pieces and resin to overlap the previous layers. Try to maintain even coverage of the laminate over the surface.

Photo 26: ...add resin, and use a brush to work the fibers loose a bit...

Photo 24: Continue adding pieces and resin, overlapping them with center circle pieces and wetting them out.

Photo 27: ...until they lay down completely and the wrinkle is gone.

Photo 25: If wrinkles develop in the mat during layup...

Photo 28: For laying up mat into odd shapes or corners, you can loosen the fiber in the mat so it will lay down sufficiently by pulling it apart or tearing it...

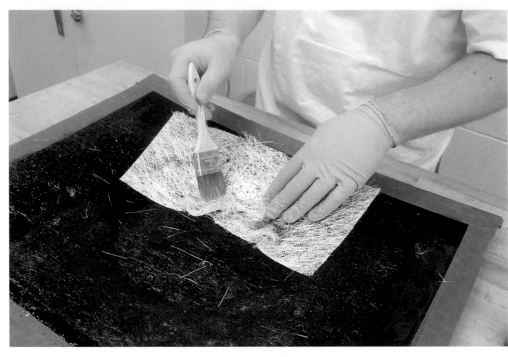

Photo 29: ...and then using a resin-saturated brush to push the fibers into place.

and bend them into various shapes to experiment with them. To demonstrate this lamination method, we will build a custom speaker panel, such as one found on a car panel or speaker box. Materials for this project include a sheet of acrylic 1/16th to 1/8th of an inch thick, 3/4" thick by one square foot medium density fiberboard (MDF), wood boards (any clean scrap wood should work well), vinylester resin and MEKP catalyst, fiberglass mat, wood glue, and some nails or screws. Tools will include saws, a hammer or screwdriver, heatgun or oven, scissors, brushes, mixing containers and applicable safety items. The lamination schedule for this project includes enough fiberglass mat to increase the thickness of the acrylic by at least 1/8th of an inch (see illustration 1), and even more near the actual speaker hole.

Acrylic sheet is available in many thicknesses and will maintain its rigidity until it is within a temperature range at which it will become pliable and formable. Thin sheets are best for forms that have tight details whereas thicker sheets are better for maintaining smooth, gradual curves. Softening of the acrylic begins at around 200 degrees Fahrenheit, but it does not become very workable until it reaches 300 to 375 degrees Fahrenheit. However, if not supported, the acrylic sheet (especially a thin sheet) may become very floppy and difficult to manage once it reaches forming temperatures. Consequently, it may be helpful to build a simple wooden frame with holes drilled in it to immobilize the edges of the sheet.

30: The completed layup will have no resin-poor (light or white) spots in it.

Acrylic comes with a protective film or paper backing on it to prevent surface scratches. Leave this paper on during any cutting or drilling operations to prevent scratching; removing scratches requires extensive, time consuming buffing. Remove this protective covering before any heating operations to keep it from igniting or permanently adhering to the surface of the acrylic.

Construct a form out of wood that you can use to help create your desired shapes. For this project, a piece of MDF works well to create a 9.5" circle that can be used to form a flat mounting surface for an 8" speaker. Cut the circular form with a band saw, sand the edges smooth, and then round over the corners of the form that will touch the hot acrylic sheet; sharp edges can grab too much or create creases and corners that are hard to fill with fiber and resin during the layup (see photos 1 and 3). A minimum of 1/4" radius works well for most forms, though even larger radii are recommended for a better layup.

After building a frame to support the acrylic sheet (see photos 4 and 5), remove the backing on the acrylic (see photo 6), securely mount it in the frame and place the frame and acrylic in an oven at 375 degrees Fahrenheit (see photos 7 and 8). If the frame is smaller than the oven's rack, place wooden supports under the frame to prop up the acrylic and keep it from sagging and touching anything (especially the heating elements) once it gets warm. Thin acrylic sheets will heat up much faster than thicker ones; so check its pliability every couple minutes by touching it from beneath with a leather-gloved hand (see photo 9). When it is ready

Photo 31: Once the composite has fully cured (after at least 24 hours), remove the masking tape...

Photo 32: ...and peel off the protective plastic film.

Illustration 33: Lamination schedule for the mandrel layup of a decorative carbon fiber motorcycle triple-clamp sleeve.

Mandrel Lamination Schedule

Resin System: Polyester or Epoxy

2 Layers - Fiberglass Sleeve (light weave)

2 Layers - Carbon Fiber Sleeve (light weave)

Photo 34: *If the tube for your mandrel needs more smoothing than wet-sandpaper can offer, a machine lathe can work wonders.*

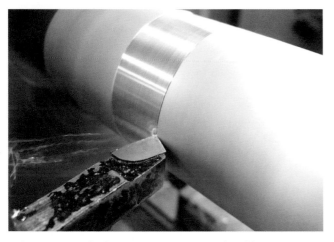

Photo 35: *A lathe can remove considerably more surface material than hand sanding…*

Photo 36: *…and it can also produce a very smooth surface.*

Photo 37: *Emery cloth (320 to 600 grit) can further smooth the lathe-turned surface…*

Photo 38: *…which can then be polished using rubbing compound and polish. The final mirror surface of the mandrel is now ready for layup.*

Photo 39: *Create a couple mandrel supports out of scrap wood covered in packing tape. Wax the mandrel completely with three to four coats of parting wax.*

Photo 40: Buff off the parting wax haze and repeat these waxing steps until this new mandrel has at least four coats of wax before its initial use.

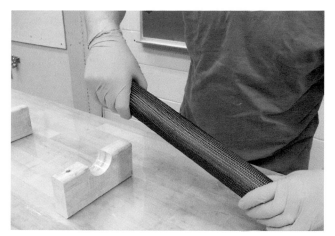

Photo 43: Smooth the weave so it lays flat on the mandrel…

Photo 41: Wrap masking tape on the mandrel's ends to keep resin off so sealant tape will later adhere to them.

Photo 44: Feel through the sleeving to find the opposite end of the mandrel, and use scissors to snip and mark the sleeve.

Photo 42: Find the proper length to cut the sleeve by sliding the dry sleeving over the mandrel.

Photo 45: Remove the sleeve from the mandrel and smooth it to the same width as supplied by the manufacturer…

Photo 46: …then cut through it with scissors.

Photo 47: Use this length as a reference to cut the other lengths of sleeve for the layup.

for forming, the sheet will have a feel similar to loose, wet leather (see photo 10). If you allow the acrylic to get too hot, bubbles will begin to form in it, and it may eventually scorch or catch fire.

Remove the hot acrylic from the oven, secure the wooden frame to a table top, press the speaker form into the warmed plastic, and position it as you desire for the shape of the surface (see photos 11-14). Unnecessarily touching the malleable plastic can introduce unsightly dimples and imperfections into the surface, so be careful not to handle the acrylic too much, but you can shape the plastic somewhat with a leather-gloved hand (see photo 15). Hold the form in place for several minutes until the plastic has cooled enough to support itself without deforming, and then remove it from the frame. Wipe any dust off the acrylic to avoid scratches and layup contaminants (see photo 16). The acrylic piece will still be somewhat flexible, though the shaping of its surface will have rigidified it more.

Using plastic film (such as a painter's drop cloth) as a barrier, tape off the front side of the acrylic to prevent inadvertent resin spills or spots (see photo 17). Cleaning resin from acrylic plastic can be a very difficult job, usually requiring considerable sanding and buffing. A little foresight at this point can save a great deal of hassle later.

Cut the fiberglass mat into various sized pieces and circles that fit the speaker's form. The pieces will lay into the form and conform to curves more easily than large pieces will, while the circles will bulk up the speaker-mounting surface. If you have a form with

Photo 48: Once the sleeve lengths are cut, wipe on or spray PVA release onto the mandrel. The mandrel and materials are now ready for layup.

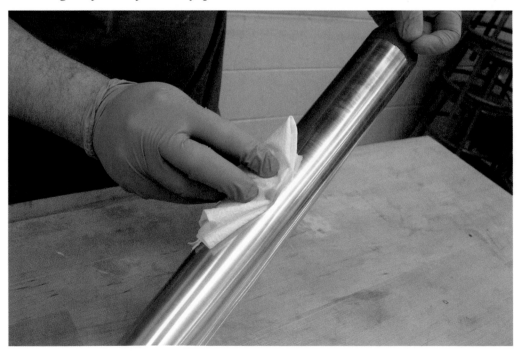

large flat sections, simply cut the mat into manageable pieces. Set aside enough mat to cover the form to the desired thickness.

The styrene in both polyester and vinylester resins will bond well to acrylic during lamination (while epoxy bonds weakly with acrylic), but vinylester tends to exhibit a slightly higher bond. For this reason, this project will use vinylester as a matrix with fiberglass mat as a reinforcement (see photo 18). Vinylester can typically be mixed by adding about 8 drops of MEKP catalyst to each liquid ounce of resin, but follow the manufacturer's recommendations for your particular resin. Prior to laminating the fabric layers to the acrylic, wipe the acrylic's surface again (see photo 19), and then completely cover all the molding surfaces with resin (see photos 20), spreading it uniformly with a blush while avoiding any resin pooling in the bottom of the acrylic form. Place some mat in the bottom of the form (see photo 21). Apply light pressure on the mat with the brush, carefully dabbing it to help workout any folds or voids in the fabric. The fibers will begin to soak up the resin brushed on the mold faces, but add resin with the brush as needed to assure saturation of the mat. As with fiberglass cloth, the mat will become transparent as the resin saturates it, so work the resin into the fibers until they are free of air bubbles and dry (white) sections.

Next, begin applying the additional strips one at a time on each of the sides of the form, then on the bottom again (see photos 22 24). Overlap these pieces to prevent voids in the laminate between the mat pieces.

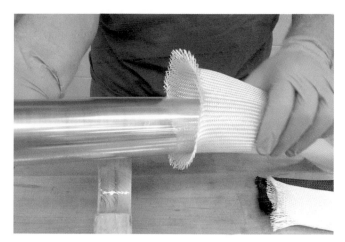

Photo 49: One method of wet layup with a mandrel includes putting the dry reinforcement over the mandrel…

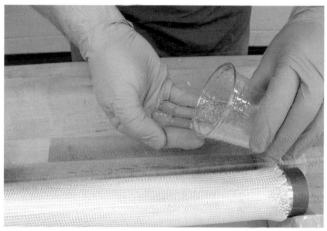

Photo 50: …smoothing out the sleeve, and pouring the resin directly in your hand or using a brush…

Photo 51: …and then applying the resin to the sleeve and working it into the weave until it is fully wetted out.

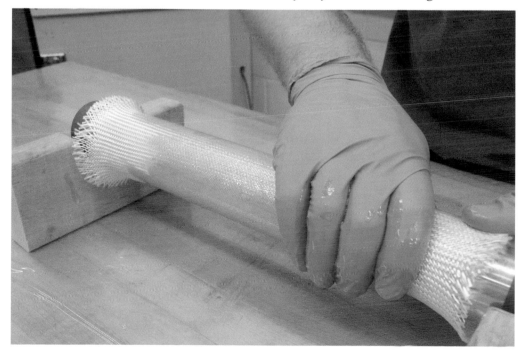

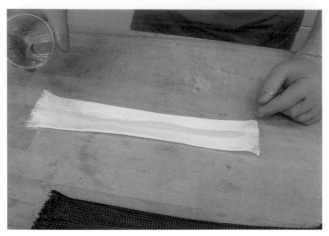

Photo 52: Another method for layup includes pouring resin over the dry sleeve while on a plastic-protected surface…

Photo 53: …using a spreader to work in the resin…

Photo 54: …opening up the sleeve's end…

Photo 55: …and sliding it over the mandrel. The resin-soaked sleeve will tend to stick to the mandrel, but it works nonetheless.

Photo 56: A variation of this previous method includes inserting one sleeve into another to minimize the hassle of sliding it onto the mandrel.

Photo 57: Pour resin over the set of sleeves…

Photo 58: ...and then work the resin into the sleeves. Squeeze the resin completely into the inner sleeves before proceeding.

Photo 61: Apply pieces of sealant tape to either end of the mandrel and take off the paper backing from only one end (for now).

Photo 59: Open the end of the sleeves and slide them onto the mandrel. "Inchworm" the sleeves down and smooth them flat onto the mandrel.

Photo 62: Stick the heat shrink tape (release-side against the composite) to the uncovered sealant tape...

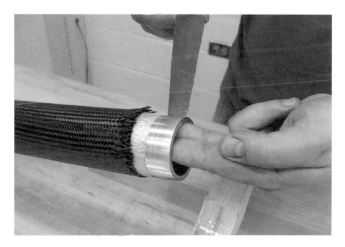

Photo 60: ...and then remove the protective masking tape at the ends.

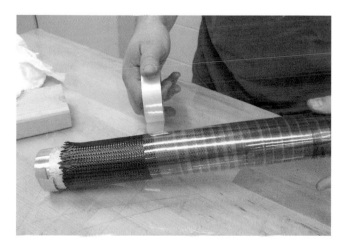

Photo 63: ...and begin wrapping it over the sleeve. Overlap the shrink tape by at least half its width, and continue until the mandrel is fully encased.

Photo 64: *Remove the protective backing on the second piece of sealant tape, adhere the heat shrink to it, and then cut the heat shrink with scissors.*

Photo 67: *Center the laminate within the shrink-tubing and begin heating the shrink tubing from one end. Rotate the mandrel for even heating.*

Photo 65: *Starting from one end, use a heat gun to warm up the tape. Keep the heat gun constantly moving to avoid overheating the composite.*

Photo 68: *...down the mandrel to evenly heat the tubing all the way to the end.*

Photo 66: *An alternative heat shrinking method is to use specialty heat shrink tubing.*

Photo 69: *When finished, you'll be able to see the heat shrink tubing tightly contracted over the laminate.*

"Moldless" Composite Lamination Schedule

Resin System: Epoxy

10 Layers - 6 oz. Fiberglass, Plain Weave
(Fibers Randomly Oriented)

Photo 70: Lamination schedule for a moldless composite hood scoop.

Photo 73: Trace the top profile of the scoop onto cardboard or poster board.

Photo 71: Cut curves into the top edges of some MDF pieces to closely match the bottom front and rear curvature of the existing scoop (or hood).

Photo 74: Quick sketches, like these created by a student who had a special interest in this project, help to guide the development of the scoop.

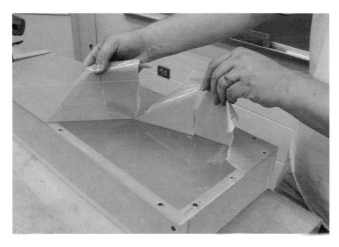

Photo 72: Screw sheet material (such as plastic or sheet metal) to these pieces to create a surface jig.

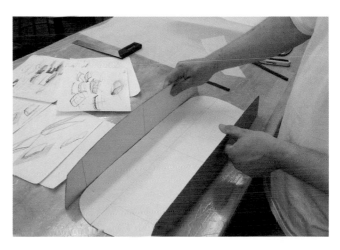

Photo 75: On the top template, measure out multiple station points for the shaping profiles and create the front and back profiles.

Photo 76: Create profiles for the mid-line and side station templates and then cut them out with a utility knife.

Photo 77: Extruded or expanded styrene foam is easily cut to size by scoring it with a sharp utility knife...

Extra resin and the brush can be used to work out bubbles (see photos 25-27), and the mat can be pulled apart or torn to help it form to curved surfaces better, as needed (see photos28 and 29). Build these layers up to match the lamination schedule, and then leave the laminated acrylic part to cure for at least twelve to twenty-four hours so it can fully harden (see photo 30). Have patience with the curing cycle, and then remove the protective plastic cover (see photos 31 and 32). The resulting composite will be considerably stiffer than the acrylic-only piece. Finally, trim the part as directed in the Finishing Techniques chapter.

MANDREL LAMINATION AND HEAT SHRINKING

"Mandrel lamination" is another simple composites molding method that can produce long, straight or tapered tubes with minimal mold complexity. A mandrel is an internal mold about which a composite is formed. This mandrel provides support for the composite until the resin in the laminate has cured. Once hardened, the mandrel can then be removed or left in the composite, depending on the needs of the application.

Mandrel lamination is used with filament wound, roll-wrapped, or sleeve-woven reinforcements. Filament winding, as mentioned previously, generally requires elaborate equipment to wind the reinforcement filament onto the mandrel, yet can produce composite vessels that are very resistant to bursting, which is why they are used extensively in forming pressure vessels.

Photo 78: ...and then applying pressure to either side of the cut over a table edge to break it in two.

Roll-wrapping is a method of simply wrapping common, flat fabric reinforcements around a mandrel and is commonly employed in the manufacture of composite fishing rods. Possibly the easiest of these mandrel lamination methods, however, involves the use of sleeve-woven reinforcements also known as "sock" or "tubing", and is typically found in the making of prosthetics. Unlike roll-wrapping, sleeve-woven reinforcements do not leave a seam from the fabric's end and will produce a slightly cleaner looking finished composite. To demonstrate this type of mandrel lamination, we will create carbon composite tube pieces from woven fiberglass and carbon fiber sleeves to be used as a cosmetic cover on the triple clamp of a street bike.

In order to create a strong, lightweight, smooth-surfaced composite, heat-shrink tape or tubing is sometimes applied on top of the composite and mandrel. Heat-shrink materials provide consolidating pressure against the composite and mandrel during the curing process and will help squeeze out excess resin and voids from the composite. Because these heat-shrink materials are somewhat specialized and only available through a few vendors, some fabricators opt for alternative methods, such as stretching and wrapping electrical tape adhesive side out around the composite and mandrel, or by using advanced vacuum-bagging techniques.

This project will require a few specialized materials and tools, some of which are available from the vendors listed in the Additional Readings and Resources. Materials include resin, woven sleeve reinforcements,

Photo 79: A handsaw can also produce a quick, controlled cut, though it will make a bit more mess.

Photo 80: If your foam is too thin for your project, it can be glued to another piece using spray adhesive.

Photo 81: Adhere the pieces with good alignment and firm pressure.

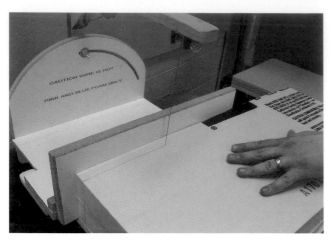

Photo 82: Square up the foam with the hot wire or saw.

Photo 85: Use the top template to guide the cuts in the foam.

Photo 83: The squared edge should be relatively straight and true. Repeat this step for the remaining three sides.

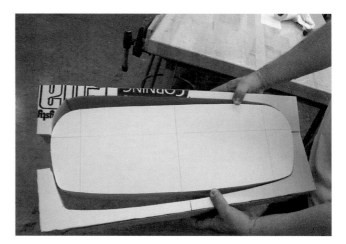

Photo 86: Cut pieces (along with the templates attached to them) so they can be refitted back onto the remaining foam block.

Photo 84: Line up and adhere the centers of the top and front templates with a center mark.

Photo 87: Rotate the foam block to view the front templates from above, and carefully cut the front profile. The remaining piece of foam should have the basic form for the hood scoop.

Photo 88: *Create straight reference lines on the bottom of the foam form based on the station lines from the front templates using a ruler.*

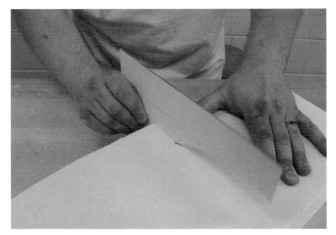

Photo 91: *…and press the mid-line template into the soft foam…*

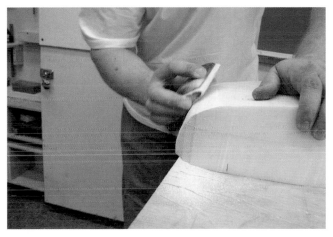

Photo 89: *Use a sanding block with 80 or 120 grit sandpaper to quickly smooth out any waves left during cutting. Check the foam's shape frequently.*

Photo 92: *…until it leaves a depression. The depth of this depression will help guide the shaping process to let you know when to stop removing material.*

Photo 90: *Bring the station line up the front and back sides of the foam with a pen or marker…*

Photo 93: *Use a shaper or rasp to quickly remove foam from the block. Once you've reached the bottom of the template's initial depression, press the template into the foam again.*

Photo 94: …using sandpaper and a block to smooth the rougher cuts out of the surface as you get closer to the final template shape.

Photo 95: The final surface should match the profile of the template.

straight metal tubing or rod of the correct inner diameter (in this case, about 2"), masking tape, heat shrink tape or heat shrink tubing, silicone tape or mastic tape, scrap wood, metal polish, wet-sandpaper, and mold release. Tools needed for this project are mixing supplies, a heat gun, scissors, a utility knife or seam ripper (from a fabric store) and, if necessary, a machine lathe. The lamination schedule for this layup includes two layers of fine fiberglass sleeve followed by two layers of fine carbon fiber weave in the width required to fit over the mandrel (see photo 33).

To get started with this project you will need to make sure the mandrel's surface is very smooth to ensure good release of the composite. If there are any minor imperfections on the surface, such as light oxidation or fine nicks, use 320 grit wet-sandpaper to smooth the surface and then sand the surface to progressively finer grits (up to at least 600 grit) until it has a near mirror surface. Avoid sanding the mandrel too much in one spot as this may create a low spot that will be hard for the composite to release from. Metal polish works well to further increase the surface smoothness and can be rubbed over the well-sanded surface (by hand or with a buffing machine) to create a fine mirror-like surface. If you intend to use tubing or rod that has large nicks in it (such as what may be found on a piece of worn, scrap tubing), use a machine lathe to turn it down until it has a smooth surface, then finish the surface with fine emery cloth and metal polish (see photos 34-38). Avoid using any tubing or rod that is dented or deeply gouged; it may take more

Photo 96: To further shape the lower profiles at the sides of the form, press the side profile template into the foam, just as with the middle profile, and finish shaping and sanding the foam to match the side profiles. The finished top shape should be smooth and match the templates as closely as possible.

work to make it usable than it is worth.

Make some supports for the ends of the mandrel out of scrap wood. This can aid in the layup of the laminate by keeping it suspended above the tabletop and also allows the mandrel to be rotated while working resin into the reinforcement. Cover the mandrel supports with packing tape to keep resin from adhering them to the mandrel.

If using the mandrel for the first time, apply at least three to four coats of paste wax, buffing it between coats (see photos 39 and 40). Tape around the ends of the mandrel with masking tape; this will keep the ends of the mandrel free from resin so the silicone or mastic tape will still stick to the mandrel prior to winding the heat shrink over the composite (see photo 41).

Next, prepare the reinforcement sleeves for layup by cutting them to size. Sleeve reinforcements can stretch or contract in length depending on how wide the diameter of the sleeve is opened — a property that makes their length difficult to determine. To find good approximate sleeve lengths, pull some sleeving over the mandrel, smooth it down, and mark its length with either a marker or a snip of the scissors (see photos 42-44). Remove it from the mandrel, cut it with scissors, and then stretch the sleeving back to its originally supplied diameter (see photo 45). Use this piece as a guide to help cut the remaining sleeve pieces (see photos 46 and 47). You can now finish preparation for the layup by coating the mandrel in PVA and then setting it on the wood supports to let it dry (see photos 48). Putting

Photo 97: *To create a sharp contour on the top edge of the scoop, create a contour line at the front...*

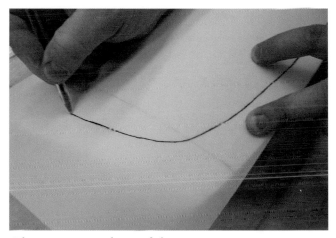

Photo 98: *...and top of the scoop.*

Photo 99: *Sand the corner down to these lines to develop the beveled front edge, as designed.*

Photo 100: Continue shaping the foam, adding a slight recess and lip in the front of the scoop until you are pleased with the form.

Photo 101: Sand the form's bottom to match the hood's curvature with 80 grit sandpaper adhered to the surface jig.

Photo 102: Once complete, peel off the sandpaper and remove the adhesive with naphtha. Trace the top profile on the surface jig.

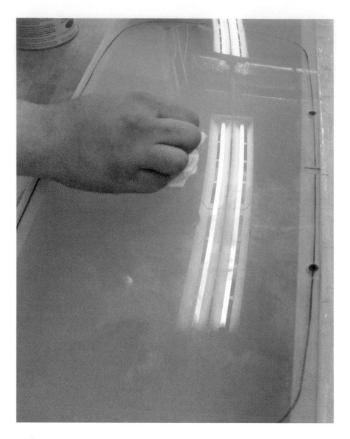

Photo 103: Apply four coats of parting wax to completely protect the surface, buffing it between coats.

on the PVA after sizing the sleeves helps avoid any tearing of the PVA that may occur by handling it too much.

Mix the resin for the lamination as instructed by the manufacturer and begin the layup. Multiple wet-out methods are possible with mandrel lamination, so a couple variations will be shown. One method involves placing a dry sleeve over the mandrel and then wetting it out with resin. To accomplish this, slightly compress and slide the first reinforcement fabric sleeve over the mandrel, carefully stretching it until it sits smoothly on the mandrel's surface. Avoid twisting the sleeve over the mandrel as twisted or uneven sleeving will have poor final aesthetics. Keep the ends of the sleeve away from the tape at the ends. Pour a little resin into your hand and work it into the fiberglass sleeve or use a brush to daub it with resin until it has become completely wetted out (see photos 50 and 51). Rotate the mandrel as needed to keep resin from creating drips off the bottom of laminate. Repeat this step with the additional layers, carefully pulling each layer

Photo 104: Cover over any screw heads in the surface using modeling clay to keep resin from filling them during layup and use a spreader or putty knife to level the clay flat with the surface.

over the previous one so it will not be disrupted.

Another lamination method for sleeves includes pouring resin over the dry sleeve, working resin into it with a brush or spreader, opening up the weave a bit, and then pulling it over the mandrel (see photos 52-55). If the resin is thin or the weave is broad enough for the resin to be worked into multiple layers at once, one sleeve can be placed inside another and wetted out prior to placing it over the mandrel (see photos 56-59).

Once the lamination is complete, it should be consolidated with the heat shrink tape or heat shrink tubing. Prior to applying heat shrink tape, peel the masking tape off the ends of the mold to reveal the mandrel's clean, waxed surface (see photo 60). If any resin has worked itself under the tape, wipe it clean so the silicone tape will properly adhere to the surface. Wrap silicone or mastic tape around each end of the mandrel, leaving the backing on the tape at one end of the mandrel (to avoid resin spills on it), and attach the shrink tape to the silicone tape (see photo 61). Heat shrink tape commonly has release on only one side, so

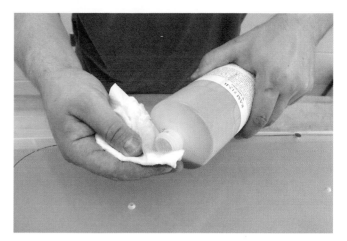

Photo 105: Wipe or spray on a film of PVA over the waxed surface.

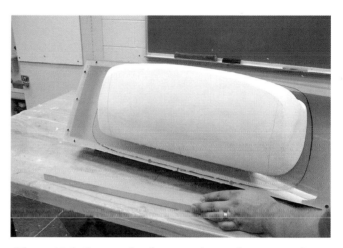

Photo 106: Secure the form to the surface jig with screws or double-sided tape.

Photo 107: Use a light satin weave for areas of tight curves, like the ones at the scoop's front.

Photo 108: Add heavier fabric over the satin weave to quickly increase the build-up of the laminate.

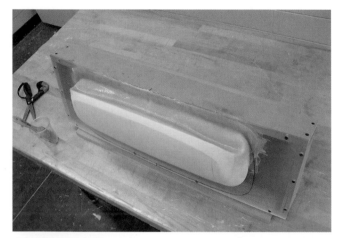

Photo 109: Allow this to cure to a tacky state, as determined by the "glove test".

make sure the release side of the tape is touching the composite. Wrap the heat shrink in a spiral up the length of the mandrel, overlapping it least 1/2 to 3/4 the tape's width (see photos 62 and 63). Remove the paper backing on the tape at the end of the mandrel, attach the heat shrink to it, and then cut the heat shrink (see photo 64).

Use the heat gun to slowly heat the shrink tape, starting from the middle of the mandrel, rotating it for even heating (see photo 65). Continue heating the tape from the middle to the ends until the tape has fully contracted and seated against the laminate. The heat shrink tape will begin to contract, squeezing out any excess resin. Make sure to use eye protection at all times during this process as the pressure created by the heat shrink tape against the laminate can cause resin to unexpectedly spurt out. Avoid holding the heat gun in one spot for too long — it may overheat and warp the shrink tape or cause bubbling in the composite.

Another method for heat shrinking the composite to the mandrel includes the use of specially treated heat shrink tubing. Heat shrink tubing will leave a slightly smoother surface than heat shrink tape will, but can be a little more expensive. If you intend to use this material, carefully slide the heat shrink over the laminate, then heat it with the heat gun from the center out, just as directed for the heat shrink tape (see photos 66-69).

Allow the composite to completely cure as directed by the resin manufacturer and then demold it as shown in the chapter on Demolding Techniques.

Photo 110: Once the resin is tacky, it should have a sufficient hold of the foam to layup the rest of the scoop. Wet-out the remaining surface of the foam and the area around the foam on the surface jig where the mounting lip will be created.

"MOLDLESS" COMPOSITE CONSTRUCTION

One method of composites creation that has been used for years on home built automobiles, boats, aircraft, sculptures, and prototypes is "mold-less" composite construction. These laminates are so named because they are made without a mold by laying the composite over a sculpted foam form, often to permanently encase the foam in it. Moldless composites are especially helpful in quickly creating one-of-a-kind parts, or for developing a plug from which a mold will be produced. Moldless parts have the added benefit of increased rigidity and impact absorption because of the foam they contain (assuming, of course, the foam is left within the composite).

Moldless composites have certain limitations that should be considered. Due to the time required to finish the surfaces of moldless composites, it is not a time-effective method for making multiple copies of a part. Additionally, you should also consider the compatibility of the resin system and foam you intend to use for moldless parts: styrene-based resins will dissolve styrene-based foams, though more expensive urethane and vinyl foams are compatible with most resin systems. If a polyester or vinylester resin is required with styrene foam, the foam can be first sealed with latex primer or paint, and then covered in the composite. Hollow composites may be created from this moldless method if styrene foam is used for the form, then dissolved out with acetone or lacquer thinner once the composite has cured.

Photo 111: Lay the first ply of fabric over the resin-soaked foam.

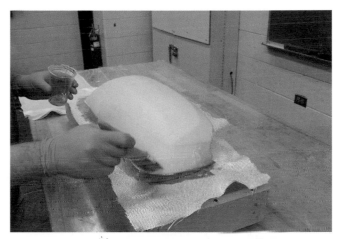

Photo 112. Add resin to the fabric until it is fully wetted.

Photo 113: ...and apply the next layer of fabric to the laminate. Wet out this layer with more resin, and continue the build-up of the laminate with successive plies.

To illustrate this particular composite fabrication method we will build a simple hood scoop for a sports car from extruded styrene foam and an epoxy-fiberglass composite. The materials you will need include pieces of extruded styrene foam (typically blue or pink in color and used for home insulation), epoxy resin and hardener, and fiberglass cloth. Needed tools include scissors, a utility knife, handsaws, foam-shaping rasps, sandpaper (80 and 120 grits) and a sanding block, brushes, mixing supplies, applicable safety equipment, and a hot-wire machine (if available). The lamination schedule for this project includes about ten layers of 6 ounce fiberglass cloth (see illustration 70).

Prepare for shaping the hood scoop by first creating a support surface to work on that approximates (as closely as possible) the actual curvature of the hood it will mount on to ensure a good final fit (see photos 71 and 72). Next develop sketches of the new hood scoop and then set up a system of templates to guide the development of this shape (see photos 73 and 74). Cut out poster board or thin cardboard to form guides for this shape (see photos 75 and 76). Avoid complex shapes with too much detail; it will be difficult to adhere the laminate to sharp corners or edges, and

small details may be totally obscured by the composite. Also, if you are designing an enclosed shape, note that it is difficult to completely encase a foam piece on all sides unless one side is first laid up and cured to a tacky state, then turned over and finished with a second layup.

Styrene foam can be cut and broken to rough size with a utility knife, or it can be cut with a handsaw (see photos 77-79). If your foam is too thin for use with your shape, it can be laminated to additional sheets with spray glue (see photos 80 and 81). Cut off any excess foam to make the shaping steps easier (see photos 82 and 83).

To use the templates as a guide for the hot wire or handsaw while shaping large profiles, align the templates with the station markings on each of them, and then adhere them to the correct sides of the foam with spray glue (see photos 84-87). Transfer alignment markings from the templates onto the foam as needed to properly locate each additional guide template (see photo 88). Next, continue to use the additional templates as necessary to guide your development of the shape while removing material with a handshaper or rasp. Follow this rough shaping with sandpaper and a block to further smooth the shape (see photos 89-101). Note that for other applications it may be easier to simply adhere foam to the template sections and then remove the foam until the sections are visible. With this particular demonstration we will be dissolving the foam after layup, so shaping sections are applied externally with removable templates to avoid them from interfering with the foam during the dissolving process. Once you've arrived at the desired shape, you are ready to mount the foam to the support surface and prepare it for lamination (see photos 102-106).

Photo 114: While still wet, cut off any excess fabric that prevents the laminate from completely laying against the surface. Apply a final extra coating of resin to the laminate to minimize sanding and finishing time before painting.

Use scissors to cut the fiberglass cloth for the lamination, and then stack them as listed in the lamination schedule for layup. Add relief cuts to the dry fabric anywhere it will not lay down on the surface well enough. Mix the epoxy resin as recommended by the manufacturer and then use a brush to completely wet the surface of the foam (see photo 107). Carefully place the first layer of reinforcement fabric onto the resin-wetted foam, avoiding any tugging of the fabric that may warp the fibers. Apply light pressure on the fabric with the brush or spreader to help work the resin through the fiber (see photo 108). Continue adding the remaining layers and resin to complete the layup (see photos 109-115). Depending on the shape of the form, you may need to add more relief cuts in the fabric so it will adhere to the foam without creating large voids. Overlapping the fabric at these spots will cause it to be thicker than necessary, but this can be corrected by sanding it down during the finishing stage.

Let the laminate and foam construction cure for at least twelve to twenty-four hours to allow it to fully harden. Once hardened completely, the styrene foam can be melted out with acetone to create the hollow form (note that this is not possible with urethane or vinyl foams) as instructed in the Demolding Techniques chapter. The resulting part can then be sanded and finished as shown in the Finishing Techniques chapter.

CHAPTER CONCLUSION

Depending on the size, shape, and use for a composite part, there are various composites fabrication methods that can be used. To quickly create a polished, finish composite with good surface durability, thermoformed and rigidized acrylic composites work very well. Straight, tubular composites can be made using an internal mold, or mandrel. Additionally, to quickly form a shape out of inexpensive foam and composites, especially to create hollow parts or molds, "moldless" composite fabrication is very useful.

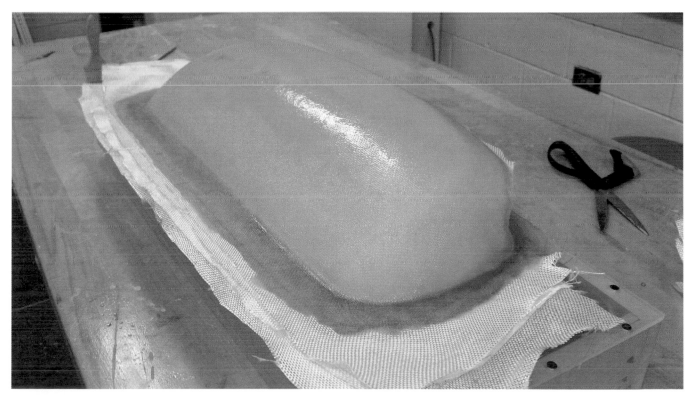

Photo 115: Allow this laminate to cure completely before demolding, trimming, and finishing it.

Chapter Seven

Demolding Techniques

Removing a Cured Part from a Mold

Most composites formed in a mold will need to be removed, or "demolded", but the shape of the particular part will determine what methods are best used to demold it. Parts that get stuck in a mold may require extra planning or even extreme demolding methods.

DEMOLDING PREPARATION

Before demolding a part, it is wise to clean the work space so there will be enough room to work around the mold and approach it from all sides. Demolding large, deep, or complex components requires a great deal of patience on the part of the

Photo 1: To demold a panel, pry up a corner of the laminate with a plastic wedge...

fabricator because the part will need to be worked edge by edge, little by little to remove the part from the mold, so space should be allocated accordingly. Further, a clean workspace will also help prevent any stray uncured resin leftover from that layup from getting on the part or mold.

For some open molded composites, extra laminate that extends beyond the edge of a mold (or "flash") can be trimmed with scissors while still in the "green-cure" state. Trimming at this stage can save some time and hassle in trimming after the part has been demolded. If your part has excess flash to its edges, review the section on "Green Trimming" in the Finishing Techniques chapter and perform this trimming step prior to demolding the part.

Photo 2: ...and push the wedge between the laminate and the mold...

PART REMOVAL

In preparation to demold a composite part, be sure that the composite has achieved a full cure and is no longer tacky or even rubbery when touched. If the part is still only partially cured, it will stick to the mold or deform during demolding. The problem of demolding an incompletely cured composite will be compounded if the resin in it was not mixed completely to begin with — a problem which may cause soft spots in the laminate, or leave the composite incompletely cured and sticky.

Even after a composite

Photo 3: ...until the laminate pulls free of the mold surface.

Continued on page 106

Photo 4: *The finished, demolded panel.*

Photo 7: *...and insert plastic wedges between the part and mold surface.*

Photo 5: *Wash any PVA residue off the panel prior to trimming.*

Photo 8: *Push the wedges further into the gaps until the part comes free from the mold.*

Photo 6: *To demold a compound curved laminate, try to push the laminate away from the side of the mold using gloved hands....*

Photo 9: *The finished, demolded part.*

Photo 10: If the mandrel has bonded to the tape-covered mandrel supports, use a mallet to break them free.

Photo 11: Peel back the sealant tape at the end of the heat shrink tape...

Photo 12: ...and begin to unwind the tape from the laminate.

Photo 13: Continue peeling back the tape...

Photo 14: Until the laminate is completely uncovered.

Photo 15: Clean any excess cured resin or "flash" from the end of the laminate. This will make its removal from the mandrel much easier.

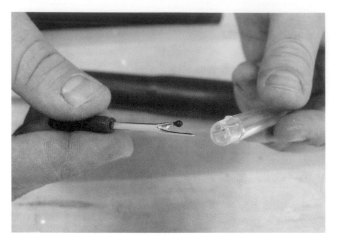

Photo 16: To remove heat shrink tubing, a seam ripper from a fabric store is very helpful.

Photo 19: …until the tubing can be pulled off the mandrel.

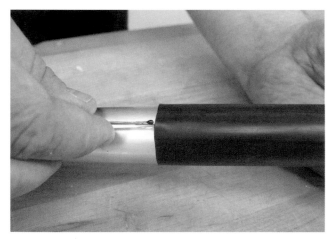

Photo 17: Push the seam ripper into the edge of the heat shrink tubing…

Photo 20: The final laminate ready to be removed from the mandrel.

Photo 18: …sliding it up the length of the laminate…

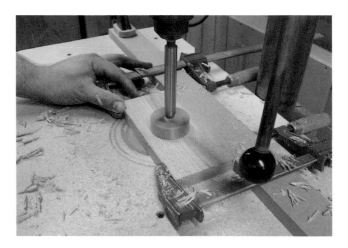

Photo 21: Make a press collet for the mandrel by drilling a hole in a piece of hard wood that matches the diameter of the mandrel.

Photo 22: A spindle sander can help to open and smooth the hole to better match the mandrel.

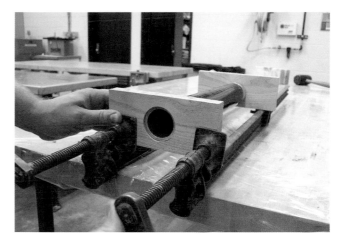

Photo 25: Tighten the pipe clamps to press the wooden collet against the laminate…

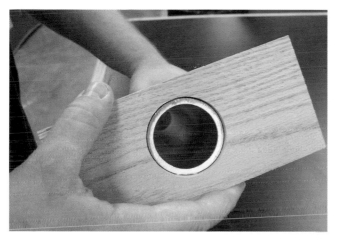

Photo 23: Test fit the wooden press collet over the mandrel to ensure a good fit.

Photo 26: …until the laminate releases from the mandrel and begins to slide down its length.

Photo 24: Butt one end of the mandrel against a board, with the other end positioned through the wooden press collet. Apply pipe clamps to the setup and make sure the system is straight.

Photo 27: Remove the laminate from the mandrel…

Photo 28: …and wash any PVA from its inner surfaces.

Photo 29: The finished laminate is ready for trimming and finishing.

part has finished curing, extracting it from a mold can still be difficult at times — in spite of a correctly designed mold. Depending on the geometry and rigidity of the part, several measures may be required to remove a molded laminate. The most effective tools for releasing a part include plastic wedges, an air nozzle and compressed air, rubber mallets, running water (for releasing PVA), and a jig or press (for mandrels or other difficult laminates).

Different means of demolding the part are available depending on the geometry of the part and the mold. The following guidelines can help determine the best method to use.

DEMOLDING FLAT PANELS

Flat or slightly curved laminates are by far the easiest parts to demold simply because they have no undercuts or complex curves that can lock them into the mold. Small panels can be removed by carefully inserting a plastic putty knife or plastic wedge between the mold and the edge of the laminate, and then slightly twisting the wedge or putty knife to sufficiently separate the panel from the mold (see photos 1-5). Larger panels can be demolded by running a plastic putty knife between the perimeter of the laminate and the mold, and then carefully inserting several wedges into the resulting voids. Rigid panels will tend to

Photo 30: Mark the location of the trim line for the hood scoop with a permanent marker.

separate from the mold all at once, while more flexible laminates may need to be released one area at a time until they can be peeled off the mold surface.

DEMOLDING COMPOUND CURVED PARTS

For composites that have large sections of compound curvature or complex mold flanges/parting lines, several techniques may be required to remove the part, depending on how voraciously the part appears to be adhering to the mold. It is advisable to start with the least intrusive demolding methods before resorting to more extreme ones.

Start by inserting a plastic-bladed putty knife between the mold and the edge of the composite, or (if there is a flange and enough flash to grasp onto) try to pry the composite away from the mold using your gloved hands (see photo 6). Never use screwdrivers or other metal implements, as they may damage the mold. Carefully drive small wedges into the gaps created by prying the composite away from the mold surfaces, avoiding any extreme flexure of the mold or composite part. In areas where the demolding seems to be working most effectively, replace the small wedges with larger ones, tapping them in with a rubber mallet until the part comes free (see photos 7-9). Be very careful about not tapping the wedges in so far that

Photo 31: *Remove the screws from the bottom of the foam and jig...*

Photo 32: *...and press a plastic wedge under the edge of the laminate to release the part.*

Photo 33: *Scrape off any clay that may have been pulled up from the jig...*

Photo 34: …and wash off any PVA residue. The part will then be ready for trimming.

they begin to break the laminate (which will be noticeable by a crunching or crackling sound).

If the part will not release with the wedges, try inserting an air nozzle or air nozzle-equipped wedge between the part and the mold. Lightly feather the air trigger to puff air into the void between the part and the mold. The part should eventually float free from the surface of the mold as air pressure pushes it up from below.

If the part is still stubbornly attached within the mold, try several moderate blows to the composite with a rubber mallet, avoiding damaging force to either the part or the mold. This may help loosen the part, making it easier for the wedges or air nozzle to take effect.

Clean the PVA film off the demolded laminate by running it under warm water and rubbing over it lightly with your hand. Allow the part to dry.

DEMOLDING A MANDREL LAMINATE

To remove the laminate formed over a mandrel, the heat shrink material laid over the laminate should be removed first. If heat shrink tape was used, carefully cut the heat shrink tape and unwrap it (see photos 10-15). At this stage, it will be very evident if the heat shrink tape was placed release-side against the laminate because it will adhere to the laminate and tear if it was not applied correctly. If any small pieces of heat shrink tape do adhere to the laminate, these can be removed

Photo 35: Once the part has been cut to the trim line (as shown in the chapter on Finishing Techniques), it is ready to have the foam within it dissolved.

with an X-Acto or utility knife blade.

To remove heat shrink tubing from a laminate, use a seam ripper tool (available at fabric stores) to cut through the tubing. Cutting the tubing in a slightly diagonal direction with the seam ripper may help it cut through the tubing more smoothly (see photos 16-20). Whether cutting heat shrink tape or tubing, avoid nicking any of the mandrel's surfaces.

To remove the laminate from the mandrel, the mandrel will need to be pressed through the laminate. A simple press system can be constructed by drilling a hole in a hardwood board (such as oak or hard maple) that matches the diameter of the mandrel, and then using bar or pipe clamps to apply even pressure on the mandrel (see photos 21- 29). When pressing out the laminate tube, it may make a slight "pop" or crackling sound as it releases and slides down the face of the mandrel. If the laminate does not quickly release from the mandrel, it may be helpful to firmly tap the laminate in several spots with a rubber mallet to loosen it. Once loose, the laminate should slide relatively easily off the end of the mandrel and may even be removed by pulling on it with your hands. Tight laminates may require use of the press system to remove them completely.

Photo 36: Acetone, a brush, and a plastic tub will be very helpful in keeping any messes to a minimum

Photo 37: Pour acetone over the foam in the moldless composite...

Photo 38: ...adding more as necessary to promote the dissolution of the foam.

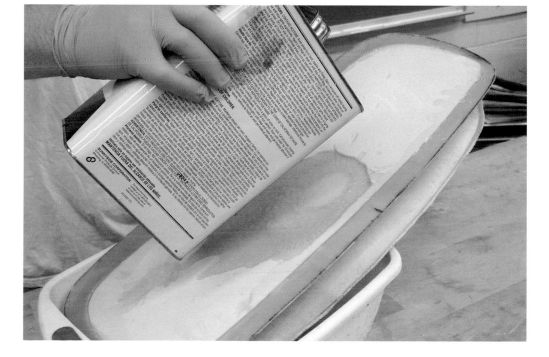

Photo 39: Continue pouring small amounts of acetone over the foam...

Photo 40: ...using a brush to wash the acetone back over the foam once it has run down it.

After removal, clean the PVA from the inside of the tubular laminate using running water, and then trim it as directed in the chapter on Finishing Techniques. Be sure to clean the mandrel after use by scraping off any excess cured resin using a small piece of scrap acrylic or other hard plastic. Never use metal implements to clean a metal mold since they can gouge or damage the mold surface.

DEMOLDING A "MOLDLESS" PART

Moldless parts that are made by laminating a composite over styrene foam can be "demolded" by dissolving away the styrene foam using acetone or styrene monomer liquid (see photos 30-45). Styrene foams break down quickly when exposed to some solvents, which can be beneficial if they need to be removed from the composite part. Care should be taken when using any solvent to dissolve the styrene, though, as solvents present health and disposal risks. Once the solvent has eaten away the styrene foam, it will leave behind a gooey mess that resembles a misplaced internal organ from a horror movie. This remaining mess will stay sticky and soft for several days (or weeks) until the solvent evaporates from it and leaves a hard mass of styrene plastic. The speed of this solvent evaporation depends on the amount of foam and solvent mixture, how thin it has been spread

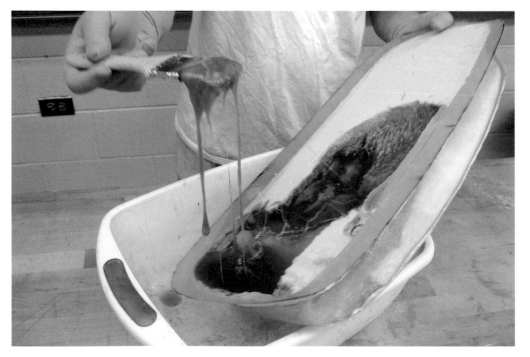

Photo 41: The foam will dissolve into a soft mess of styrene plastic.

out, how much air is flowing over the mess, and the ambient air temperature.

Unfortunately, this method of melting out the moldless composite's foam structure does not work for all foams. Urethane or vinyl foams are made from more chemically resistive plastics and will not simply dissolve as styrene will. They can, however, be laboriously chiseled and scraped out of the composite, though this is a very time intensive way to remove these types of foams.

DEMOLDING COMPOSITE TOOLING FROM A PLUG

Even with the correct wax/PVA release protection, a composite mold will appear to be solidly adhered to the plug and flange form surfaces over which it was laminated. To remove the mold, carefully slide a plastic wedge under one edge of the laminate, between the laminate and the mold itself. Push the wedge into the seam with steady pressure to help open up the gap and remove the mold (see photos 46-56). Again, be very careful not to gouge the mold with the sharp edges and corners of any hard, sharp objects.

If the mold does not immediately release from the plug, slowly push in additional plastic wedges into the void between the mold and the flanges.

Continued on page 114

Photo 42: Continue to add acetone...

Photo 43: ...breaking off pieces as it eats away at the foam.

44: Continue to remove foam residue...

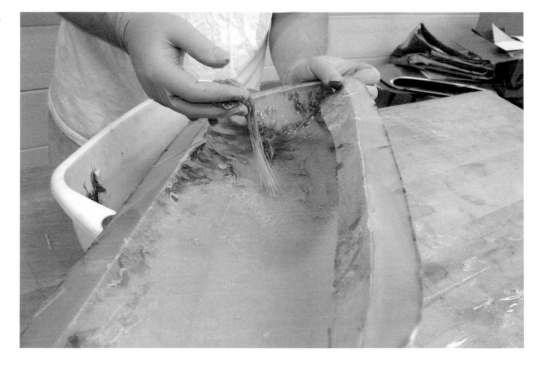

Photo 45: …and use a scrubbing pad to further clean the surface with acetone until it is free of the styrene foam or styrene plastic residue.

Photo 48: …ensuring a clean cut by using a sharp carbide drill bit.

Photo 46: To demold composite tooling, as with this two-part fender mold, begin by removing any of the flange forms left on the mold.

Photo 49: Drill enough alignment holes to adequately hold the removable mold section in place once hardware has been inserted through them.

Photo 47: With multi-part molds, drill alignment holes prior to demolding the mold sections from the plug…

Photo 50: Drive plastic wedges between the mold section and the plug…

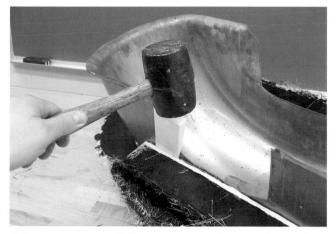

Photo 51: ...carefully tapping on them with a rubber mallet...

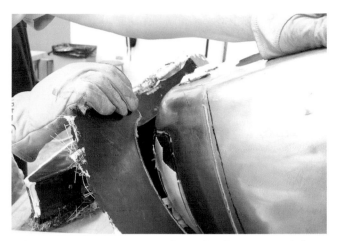

Photo 54: Continue to pull on the flanges until the mold comes free of the plug...

Photo 52: ...until the mold section releases from the plug.

Photo 55: ...and the two can be separated completely.

Photo 53: If possible, pull on the flanges of the mold with gloved hands to release it from the plug.

Photo 56: The resulting high-quality mold surfacs formed from the plug are evident in this photo of the demolded composite tooling.

Photo 57: If you encounter a part that is difficult to release, attempt to use plastic wedges first.

Photo 58: Try carefully (but firmly) tapping on the outside of the mold where the seized part is located, in an attempt to free it from the mold.

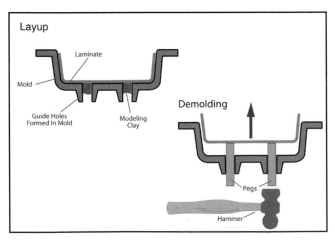

Illustration 59: Some molds may be designed to contain holes for dowels that can act as ejection pins to help remove deep, troublesome parts.

Work the wedges around the edge of the mold until it releases. If the mold still won't release, try creating a removal jig (as explained below).

Once demolded, clean the PVA film off the released mold by running it under warm water and rubbing over it lightly with your hand. Allow the part to dry, and then trim as directed in the chapter Finishing Techniques.

REMOVING "PROBLEM" PARTS

Occasionally, a part will not release from a mold as planned. This can often be frustrating, especially when expensive composite materials were used in the part's layup and there may be the chance that extreme removal steps will damage either the laminate or the mold. In the process of removing a stubborn part, however, always start with the least invasive removal methods first (see photos 57, 58).

If, at the beginning stages of part and mold design, it is evident that the part may have a difficult time releasing from a mold because of its geometry, holes can be create in the bottom of the composite tooling to allow the use of dowels or pegs for demolding. During layup, these holes should be plugged with modeling clay to prevent the seepage of resin from out of the mold. Once the laminate has cured, clean the clay from the holes with the tip of a flat blade screwdriver. Insert dowels or pegs into the holes and carefully tap on them with a hammer (see illustration 59). This action should help release the part from the mold walls without much hassle.

Plugs or composite parts that have considerable thickness to them can sometimes be removed by fabricating a make-shift removal jig that employs large-threaded screws to extract the seized component from the mold (see illustration 60). Sturdy wood or scrap metal tubing that is braced against the mold flanges work well for this purpose. Drill holes in the wood or metal that will allow screw threads to pass through them, and then tighten the screws into the jammed material until they begin to pull it out (see photo 61).

When less extreme methods fail to remove a stuck part, you may need to resort to destructive tactics to remove the part. It is usually best to sacrifice the part rather than the mold, simply because molds generally take more time, effort, and expense to build than the laminates that go in them. Carefully chip away at the part, little by little, with a flat blade screwdriver or chisel, paying very close attention that you do not drive the tool too deep into the material and mar the surfaces of the mold (see photos 62, 63). If necessary, use the edge of a plastic wedge to pry against rather than directly contacting the mold as you tear through the trapped part. After removing all the pieces, inspect the mold for damage and make repairs as needed.

Chapter Conclusion

Demolding a panel is a relatively simple task requiring the simple use of plastic wedges. Complex curved parts and composite tooling can be a bit more difficult to demold, requiring more work with plastic wedges and prying with gloved hands. Mandrel laminations require the use of a press system, while "moldless" parts can be separated from their forms with solvent.

Photo 61: Boards with through-holes drilled in can be used to create a removal jig. Here, screws are passed through and tightened into the plug section that is stuck in the mold in an attempt to pull the piece out.

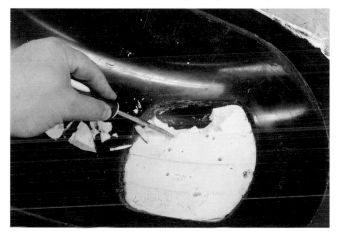

Photo 62: If a removal jig still will not release a part, it may be necessary to break it out. Use a flat-blade screwdriver or small chisel to carefully fracture and remove pieces of the part.

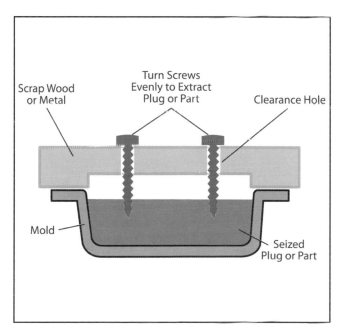

Illustration 60: An example of a part or plug removal jig.

Photo 63: Continue removing pieces of the part until it is completely free from the mold.

Chapter Eight

Finishing Techniques

Trimming and Completing a Composite Project

Before producing precision cuts on a composite, it is generally best to remove off any excess material that may be hazardous or troublesome during the final trimming process. To finish a part, additional components may be secondarily bonded to it, rough surfaces may be sanded and filled, and coats of cosmetic paint or resin may be applied to make it more presentable.

TRIMMING DEMOLDED PARTS

Composite parts are usually designed to be laid-up so that material extends past the edge of the mold. This allows the part to be trimmed to a clean edge of uniform thickness after demolding. Following these simple steps will help ensure the clean trimming of composite parts.

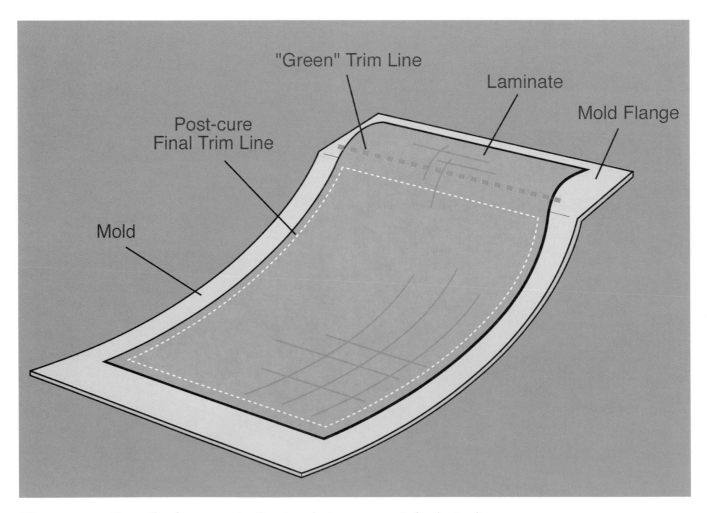

Illustration 1: Example of a green trim line in relation to a part's final trim line.

"Green" Trimming

If your part has been laid-up in an open mold where the edges of the mold are accessible during cure, it may be possible to trim part of the composite while still in the mold (see illustration 1). When the resin composite is cured to gel-like state (evident by its heavy viscosity while still being tacky to the touch) the fibers are nearly completely immobilized, but can be easily trimmed with a utility knife or scissors because the resin is still soft. Excess fabric reinforcement can be carefully removed at this stage, taking special caution to not disturb the laminate or deform it from the sides of the mold. Trimming at this stage will reduce the number of rough, sharp edges and make the part easier to handle after demolding. However, a word or caution: if physical tearing of the laminate bonds occurs during green trimming, it will be evident by the resin crumbling into small rubbery bits and by separation of the laminate plies — damage that is very difficult, if not impossible, to repair on most parts.

When green trimming a part, avoid cutting off all the flash on the part's edge. Leaving at least some flash on the part in the mold (from 1/2 to 1 inch of material) will provide the fabricator with a little leverage to push back the edge of the part and insert wedges down the mold side during demolding.

Pre-trimming & Cleaning a Composite Part

After demolding, a composite may have several hazardous edges or hardened threads that need "pre-trimming" before they can be handled safely and the part can be trimmed more accurately. Wear leather or canvas gloves to protect your hands when handling such edges; they can be extremely abrasive and can cut through skin very easily. Use sheet metal snips or hand shears to cut off any protruding stray fibers and jagged material at edges that may be dangerous during final trimming (see photos 2-3).

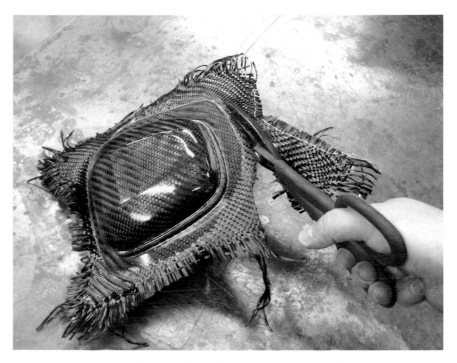

Photo 2: Pre-trimming a part can be done using metal shears.

Photo 3: A pre-trimmed part ready for final trimming.

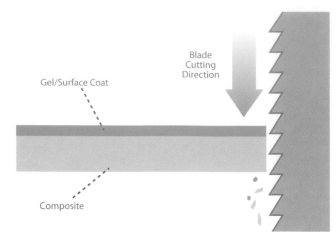

Photo 4: Example of cutting a gel-coated laminate.

Photo 7: Continue cutting through the laminate with the hacksaw until the edge is trimmed as desired.

Photo 5: To make a straight cut on a panel, a scratch awl and a ruler can be used to strike a guide-line for cutting.

Photo 8: The resulting edge will be a bit rough, but can be sanded later.

Photo 6: Begin cutting the panel with a hacksaw, cutting into the gel coat side of the laminate with the down-stroke of the hacksaw.

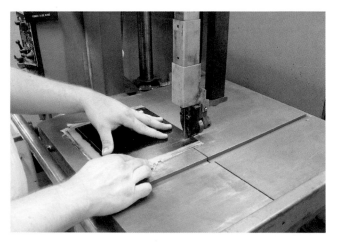

Photo 9: If cutting a gel-coated laminate with a bandsaw, make sure to cut it with the blade pushing into the gel-coat, similar to using a hacksaw.

Photo 10: Before trimming a rigidized acrylic part with a jigsaw, tape off the surfaces that may be scratched by coming into contact with the feet of the jigsaw.

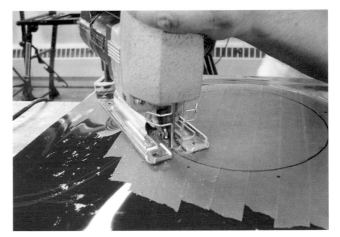

Photo 13: Guide the jigsaw around the part, following the trim line...

Photo 11: Use a template to trace the outline of the speaker and mounting holes for this demonstration part.

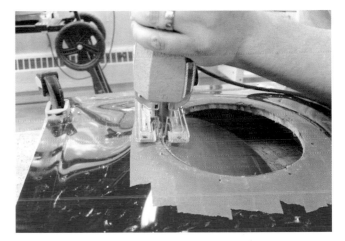

Photo 14: ...until the unwanted material is removed.

Photo 12: Drill a pilot hole through which the jigsaw can be inserted to start cutting.

Photo 15: Finish trimming the part by drilling the mounting holes.

Photo 16: To trim the hood scoop, make sure the trim line is positioned correctly by aligning and tracing the original top profile template.

Photo 17: Use a rotary tool and a cut-off wheel to make the straight cuts on the scoop...

Once the unsafe fibers have been removed, it is helpful to also wash off any PVA film that is on the laminate. Demolded parts often pick up at least a little of the protective PVA release film from the mold surface, but this film is very easily removed by running it under warm water and rubbing it lightly with your hands or a dishwashing scrubbing pad. Removing this film will make the part a little easier to handle because the PVA film can otherwise tend to stick to sweaty hands or attract dust during other trimming operations.

TRIMMING THE PART

A few methods for trimming are possible, depending on the type of composite and its geometry. The following guidelines can help determine the best method to use:

Hacksaw – Best used for trimming small parts that only need straight or large diameter curves cut in them. Since a hacksaw can be laborious and time consuming, this method is generally avoided unless it is needed for small cuts. Additionally, gel coated surfaces may chip when the teeth of the blade push the gel coat away from the laminate, so make sure the blade is oriented with the teeth pushing into the gel coat side of the composite first (see illustration 4, and photos 5-8). Carbide hacksaw blades will last much longer when trimming composites.

Bandsaw (Fine-tooth Carbide-blade) – Best when trimming flat, medium-size parts with straight or large diameter edge contours (see photo 9). Bandsaws are excellent for cutting parts quickly, though they may have similar problems as hacksaws when cutting gel

Photo 18: ...and make several small straight cuts at the corner to approximate the curves at the corners. Corners can be smoothed later with a file and sanding block.

coated parts. Non-carbide blades with wide teeth may spark when cutting composite parts and consequently dull very quickly.

Jigsaw – Can be used similarly to a bandsaw, but best for parts that have cuts confined to the middle of the part rather than around its edges (see photos 10-15). Again, use carbide blades with a jigsaw.

Rotary Tool and Abrasive Cut-off Wheel – Best for trimming flat or slightly curved surfaces with straight or large diameter curves (see photos 16- 9). Air-powered and electric (Dremel) versions are available, but both require the use of a dust mask or respirator. Air-powered types work well at blowing the trimming dust from the edge as it cuts, while electric types work best where a compressed air supply is not available. Care should be taken to avoid too much friction from the cutting wheel at the trim site because excess heat produced by the spinning wheel will break down the resin and weaken the composite.

Rotary Tool and Rotary File – Best used when trimming highly curved surfaces or tight radius curves (see photos 20-22). Rotary files work well with small to large parts, but may be time consuming for larger trim jobs. Less straight-line control is possible with this tool, so additional edge finishing may be necessary after trimming. This tool is not recommended for trimming aramid composites because aramid fibers will fill the teeth of the rotary file and minimize cutting efficiency.

Abrasive Water-jet Cutter – Best used for cutting aramid fabrics, thick lamminates, or when performing mass-production runs of a part. Manual and CNC versions are available, but water-jet cutting can be

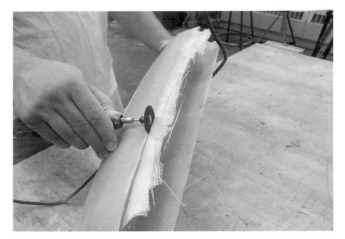

Photo 19: Trim off additional material as needed to further clean up the part.

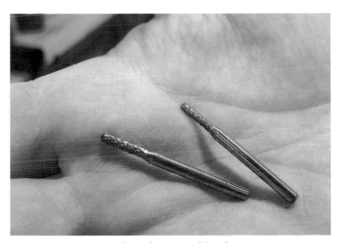

Photo 20: Examples of rotary files for use in a rotary tool.

Photo 21: Rotary files can be used to make tightly curved cuts.

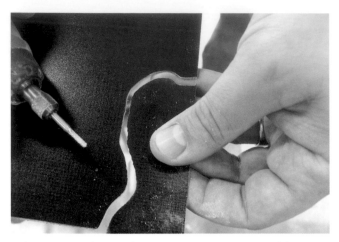

Photo 22: The resulting curvaceous cut possible with a rotary file.

Photo 23: Sanding the edge of a panel laminate using an MDF board with sandpaper glued to it.

extremely cost prohibitive for small-scale composite applications. However, it is useful in maintaining clean edges on all types of composites.

CNC Router – Best for trimming production parts where aramid fabrics are not used. Three-axis versions work well for most planar or slightly contoured parts, while five-axis versions are required for parts with complex trim lines and large or bulky contours. CNC trimming is most cost effective when used in situations where tool paths and program changes are infrequent (such as with large production runs). Carbide bits should be used to prolong the useful life of the bit while cutting composites.

FINISHING TRIMMED EDGES

As trimmed edges (especially those trimmed by hand) can often be jagged and unsightly, filing and sanding is recommended to further smooth out the part's edges. Filing with a metal file can help level unevenly trimmed edges very quickly (see photos 23-31). After filing, either wet or dry sanding will work, but wet-sanding produces far less hazardous (and annoying) dust. Using a block, a piece of high grit wet-sandpaper, and a wet sponge, water-filled basin, or running water, work over the trimmed edge until the final edge dimensions and shape are achieved. Apply water to the composite as needed to float any sanded debris away. This may take considerable time, depending on the quality and accuracy of the trimmed edge. Once it has been trimmed and the edges finished, the part is then ready for secondary bonding, surface treatments, or immediate use.

Photo 24: Using a sanding block to smooth the edge of a laminate.

Preparing Composite Tooling
for Layup

New composite tooling requires a bit of preparation before it can be used to produce parts. The composite mold may have modeling clay still attached to it from the sealing fillets and gap filling performed earlier, or it may have small areas of flashing from gel or surface coat that seeped into cracks during layup. Use a rag to wipe this excess clay from the mold, then use soap or naphtha to remove the clay residue. If necessary, use acetone sparingly to further clean areas of the mold that may have stubborn residues on them.

Use wet sandpaper to remove any blemishes in the mold, such as scratches or material left by the plug. Larger blemishes can be smoothed with a fine-tooth file (see photos 32-33). To smooth rough areas of the actual mold surface, start with a 180 or 220 grit wet-sandpaper, and then work to progressively finer grits (up to at least 600 grit) to smooth the mold (see photo 34). If you find any pores or bubbles in the mold surface, grind them out with a rotary tool and fill them with tooling gel coat or epoxy surface coat. Allow these spots to cure, then sand them smooth again using wet-sandpaper (see photos 35-40).

Trim the mold and mold flanges with either a hacksaw or a Dremel with a cut-off wheel or rotary file attached (see photos 41-45). As your trim lines will most likely be wavy and rough, use a file to level down the edges, and then wet-sandpaper the edges smooth using a block to keep the final edges clean.

Photo 25: The sanded, smoothed edge of a panel laminate.

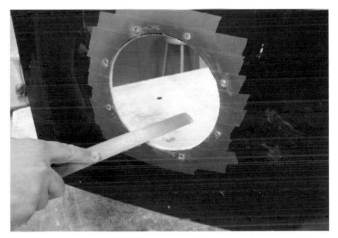

Photo 26: A metal file can quickly remove material at the trimmed edge of a laminate...

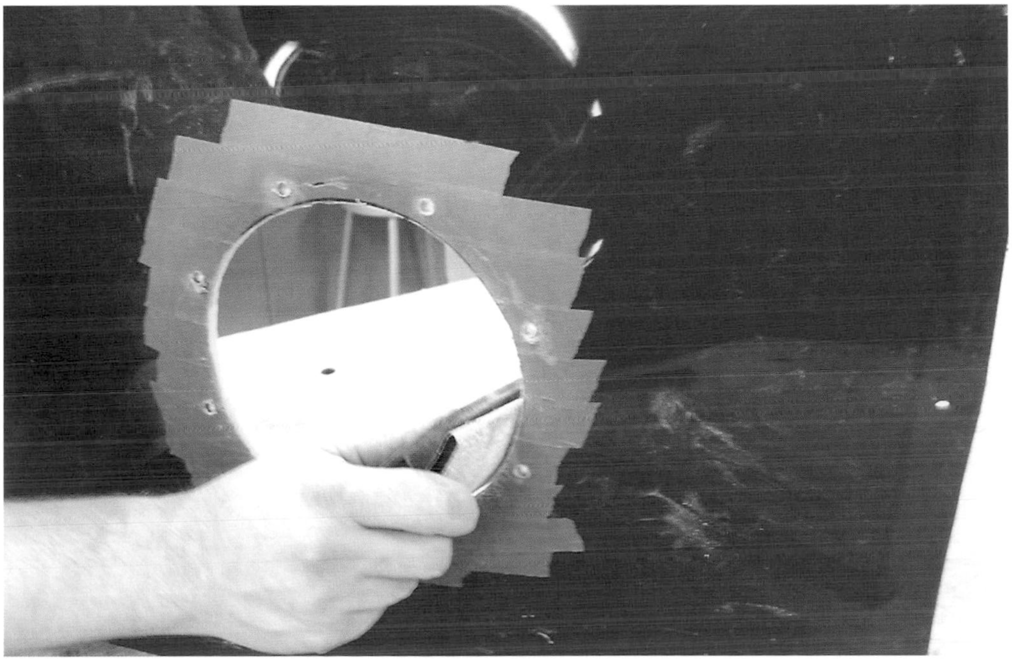

Photo 27: ...and the resulting edge can be easily sanded with a sanding block.

Photo 28: *A spindle sander will speedily smooth holes in a laminate, but be careful to avoid overheating the composite by using moderate pressure and new sanding drums whenever possible.*

Photo 31: *…and a speaker mounted in the rigidized acrylic part.*

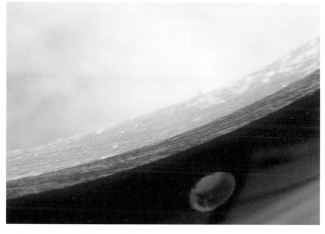

Photo 29: *The resulting smooth edge of the trimmed and sanded rigidized acrylic part.*

Photo 32: *Use a metal file to smooth any sharp corners left during the molding of composite tooling.*

Photo 30: *The final part before mounting the speaker…*

Photo 33: *File away any stray or rough fibers found on the back of the mold to prevent any possible injury while using the mold in the future.*

Photo 34: Wet-sanding can further smooth out any rough areas found in the mold.

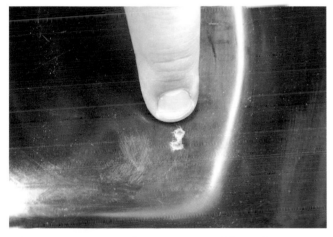

Photo 35: Damaged areas in a mold can be repaired very simply using common tools and resins.

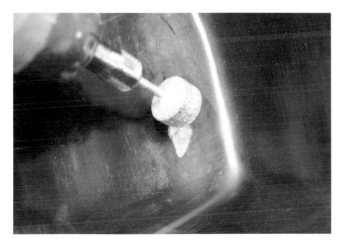

Photo 36: Grind out the damaged region of the mold to provide more surface area for the resin to lock into during the repair.

Photo 37: Apply tooling gel coat or epoxy surface coat resin into the damaged area and allow it to cure completely before smoothing it.

Photo 38: Use a small block of wood and some wet-sandpaper to carefully smooth out the filled area, while avoiding any sanding of the surrounding surfaces.

Photo 39: The fully sanded surface is barely visible in the mold.

Photo 40: *After applying cutting/rubbing compound, polishing and waxing the repaired area, the mold is ready again for service.*

Photo 41: *To trim a mold's flanges, first create trimming guidelines. Since this mold is black, a silver marker is being used for better visibility.*

Photo 42: *Use a rotary tool and a cut-off wheel to trim the flanges...*

Photo 43: *...and remove rough laminate edges.*

Photo 44: *Trim regions of the flanges as needed to produce a clean mold edge. A detail of the mold registration is shown here.*

Photo 45: *Insert alignment hardware to hold the multi-part mold sections together.*

Photo 46: *Polish all sanded surfaces of the mold and wax them in preparation for use.*

Photo 49: *Add appropriate thickeners to the bonding resin…*

Photo 47: *The finished mold is ready for service.*

Photo 50: *…until they turn the resin into a peanut butter-like paste.*

Photo 48: *Prior to secondary bonding, coarsely sand (using 36 or 80 grit) the two surfaces to be bonded together.*

Photo 51: *Spread the resin paste over the sanded areas of both parts…*

Photo 52: ...and join the parts together, aligning them as closely as possible.

Photo 53: Use a round-ended stick to scrape off any excess paste...

Photo 54: ...and allow the paste to sufficiently cure before putting the bonded parts into service.

Photo 55: Rough surfaces can be easily sanded with coarse sandpaper (120 grit) and a sanding block.

Photo 56: Laminate surfaces will generally sand down very quickly.

Photo 57: Beware of pores that may develop during sanding due to voids in the laminate...

Photo 58: ...especially if the voids are large.

Photo 61: Here, a half-round file is used to dress out a corner of the hood scoop...

Photo 59: Additional sanding can often remove such voids...

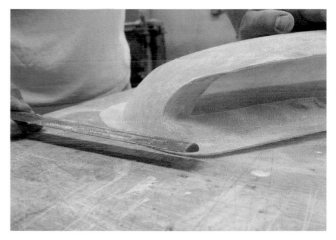

Photo 62: ...until it is shaped as needed.

Photo 60: ...but additional pores may still resurface with more sanding.

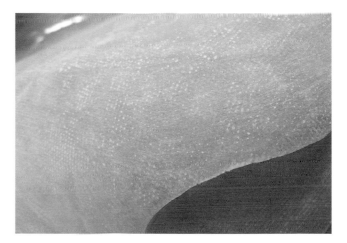

Photo 63: A close-up shows the pores in the laminate filled with dust.

Photo 64: *Use an air-hose to blow dust from the pores…*

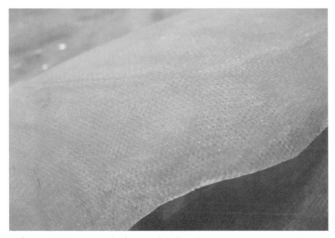

Photo 65: *…and clean the laminate in preparation for filling.*

Use cutting/rubbing compounds and polish to bring all molding and flange surfaces of the tooling to a high luster (see photos 46-47). Even small pinholes can cause problems during molding, so be sure to address and smooth out any of surface imperfections. Apply wax to all surfaces of the mold (including the backside of the mold, as this will aid in cleanup of the mold if resin spills occur) and prepare it for use.

SECONDARY BONDING

Some part designs will not allow all the needed features of a part to be molded at one time. This may require additional features (such as brackets, mounts, or even entire part sections) to be secondarily bonded onto a component after it has be molded. Secondary bonding, while not the preferred method of joining composite components, can still be effective for rigidly mounting parts to one another.

Before attempting to bond composite components to each other, prepare their bonding surfaces by sanding them with a coarse grit sandpaper or file to create sufficient "bite" for the adhesive to key into (see photo 48). Smooth surfaces will bond poorly, and may just simply release from each other instead of bonding.

Clean the sanded bonding surfaces by using high-pressure air to clear off any dust, and then wash any remaining dust residue from them with water or acetone. Mix resin (epoxy generally works most effectively for secondary bonding) with a thickener such as colloidal silica or high density filler to create a paste that has the consistency of peanut butter (see photos 49-50). Apply this adhesives mixture to the cleaned bond-

Photo 66: *To sand the surface of a tube, first cut it to length (in this case, with a horizontal bandsaw).*

ing surfaces (see photo 51). Join the parts together and clean up any excess resin paste that squeezes out the edges using a round-ended stick (see photos 52-54).

Hold (or clamp) the parts in place until the resin has cured completely (as recommended by the resin manufacturer) before putting the bonded parts into service.

SURFACE SANDING

Dry sanding composite parts can quickly remove material and smooth surface to produce high-quality parts (see photos 55-69). Electric or air-powered sanders work very well for large jobs, but simple hand sanding with a block can quickly smooth out small parts. Use coarse grits (80 and 120 grit) for very fast material removal, and then work up to finer grits (320 to 600 grit) for better surface quality. Take care when using power sanding equipment with composites; the high surface speeds of dull sanding media will cause the resin in a composite to burn and break down, producing fumes, burn marks, and overall poorly sanded surfaces.

One difficulty with sanding composites comes from the dust it produces. The microscopic fibers removed during sanding can cause work themselves into the skin, causing itchy irritation and general discomfort and airborne fibers and are hazardous in their own right (with both short and long term effects) when breathed into the lungs. For this reason, wet-sanding is the preferred method of smoothing surfaces with abrasives (see photo 70). Water will contain and float composite particles away from the sanded area,

Photo 67: If using a lathe to sand a composite tube, do not overtighten or crush it.

Photo 68: Use emery cloth sandpaper to smooth the carbon tube, but be careful not to sand too much in one spot—carbon fiber sands down very quickly!

Photo 69: The finished carbon tube ready for a resin or clear coat finish.

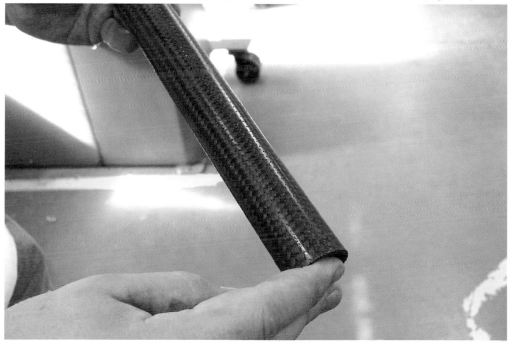

Photo 70: *Tubing can also be wet-sanded by hand, though it will take considerably longer to do.*

Photo 73: *Spread the filler onto portions of the laminate surface, applying moderate pressure to ensure that the filler squeezes into the pores completely.*

Photo 71: *To fill surface imperfections in a composite, high-quality body filler works well. Measure out correct amounts of the body filler and hardener…*

Photo 74: *Smear on the filler in small, manageable amounts…*

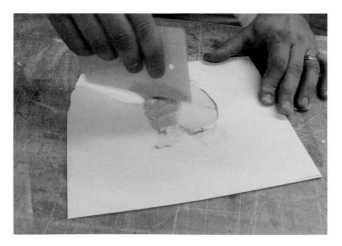

Photo 72: *…mixing the two parts together completely before applying them to the laminate's surface.*

Photo 75: *…smoothing it out as much as possible to minimize sanding effort later.*

Photo 76: Use 120 grit sandpaper to begin smoothing the filler once it has hardened completely.

Photo 77: Continue sanding the filler…

Photo 78: …constantly feeling the surface to watch out for any high or low spots that may develop as the filler is sanded down.

Photo 79: Once the surface is smoothed enough, move to another region of the part and apply more filler to it…

Photo 80: …again, smoothing it as much as possible before letting it harden. Keep sanding and filling until the surface appears and feels smooth.

Photo 81: The finished laminate may look a bit spotty, but it should end up smooth to the touch and as void-free as possible.

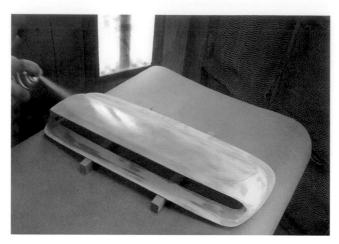

Photo 82: For small jobs, a high-quality spray can of automotive primer can be used to seal the surface of the laminate and to find any additional unseen pores.

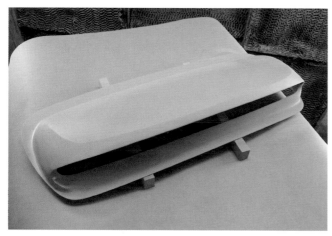

Photo 83: Completely coat the surface of the part with primer...

while at the same time keeping the composite cool so thermal breakdown of the resin is significantly minimized. Wet-sandpaper is commonly available in fine grits (from 220 to 1200 or higher), though more coarse grits are sometimes available from specialty paint suppliers.

SURFACE FILLING

Occasionally, the surface of a composite part will need to be filled due to the development of pores or surface roughness during the molding process. This is especially true of composites that are formed without touching a mold face (such as a moldless composite). To smooth these surfaces out, they will need to be filled and sanded to a good finish. This may require considerable time, but approaching this task with an attitude toward good craftsmanship will help produce very clean, presentable final parts. Use spot-putty or a small amount of automotive body filler to close any pores (see photos 71-81). Avoid applying body filler or paint directly to any styrene-based foam surfaces because solvents in these can dissolve the foam.

SURFACE FINISHING
Paint/lacquer

Apply primer to the composite that is compatible with the paint system to be used for the final coats. Fill any additional pores that may appear during these primer coats (see photos 82-86). When the primer has dried, apply a couple coats of paint (either from a can or gun) to show off the final surface.

Polyurethane

Many acrylic and urethane paints (including clear coats) provide the UV protection required to shield

Photo 84: ...and then inspect the surface closely to locate any additional pin-holes that may need to be filled with spot putty.

epoxy-based composites from damage. They are commonly available from automotive body and painting supply stores, many of which carry good information about the protection their paints can offer). These paints come in an endless variety of colors and are usually best applied with a spray gun, though for small jobs spray cans will often do an acceptable job (see photos 87-89).

RESIN/FLOODCOATING

To show off the weave of a composite (as is common with carbon and aramid-hybrid weaves), a "flood-coat" is usually in order. A flood-coat is a thick coating of resin that is either sprayed on (typical of polyester resins) or brushed over the composite and then allowed to cure. Flood-coats can produce a highly polished or "wet" surface look as they easily fill in small voids and pores, leaving a clear, smooth, level shell over the composite (see photos 90-96). Many fabricators of aftermarket automotive body panels routinely apply such coats, and frequently use UV-stabilized polyester resins over polyester-based composite parts. Flood coats can even be tinted with dyes to produce a colored translucency for special effects.

A couple drawbacks of flood-coats include the extra weight they add to a composite component, and the brittleness they give the finished surface. Flood-coats add significant weight to a composite because the resin used for these coatings tends to be much thicker than paint coats. This makes flood-coats undesirable for applications where the weight of a composite is critical, such as for competition parts.

Photo 85: Once completely primed and filled...

Photo 86: ...the part will be ready for final painting and mounting to the vehicle.

Photo 87: Spraying automotive acrylic lacquer from a can is a simple way to apply a quick clear coat to a small-scale smoothed carbon composite.

Photo 88: *The final laminate will have a high-gloss shine…*

Photo 91: *…and then blow off and clear away any dust from its surface.*

Photo 89: *…and will look right at home once it is cut to size and mounted for use.*

Photo 92: *Mix up the surface resin (in this case, a specific epoxy blend manufactured by West Systems especially for flood coating)…*

Photo 90: *In preparation for applying a flood coat, sand the surface of the composite with a coarse grit sandpaper (120 grit)…*

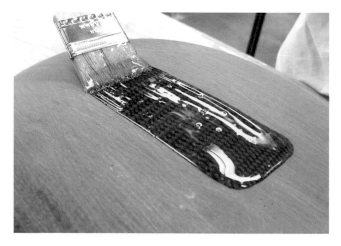

Photo 93: *And apply it in heavy amounts with a brush.*

Flood-coats also lack some important toughness that reinforced resins otherwise exhibit. Because of their lack of reinforcement, they tend to be very brittle and possess an inferior secondary bond between the cured part and the flood coat. Unfortunately, this leaves the part with a "pretty" coating that will easily chip, fracture, or separate from the composite if it is significantly impacted or flexed. These performance deficiencies are further compounded by the fact that damaged flood-coat surfaces are extremely difficult to repair, usually requiring complete sanding and removal of the affected area followed by a recoating or resin. Take these limitations into account when finishing composites so they will be able to deliver the performance you desire from them.

Photo 94: Take care to pull out as many bubbles as possible…

CHAPTER CONCLUSION

To pre-trim a composite part, excess flash from its edges can be trimmed while it is still in a "green" state, or it may be quickly removed using metal shears. To trim a part to final dimensions, a variety of hand tools or power tools are available to speed up the job and produce a clean, smooth finished edge. Surfaces can be further developed for better presentation by sanding and filling them, and by applying one or more surface treatments such as paint, polyurethane, or specially formulated coating resins.

Photo 95: …and then gingerly use a heat gun to help thin out the resin and bring any bubbles to the surface.

Photo 96: The final flood coat should have minimal imperfections, but these can be further wet-sanded (with 320 to 600 grit) from the part's surface once it has cured. Always follow epoxy resin flood coats with a UV protective clear coat.

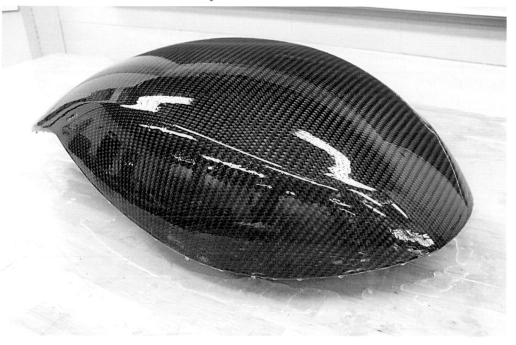

Conclusion

As a professional educator interested in teaching the fundamentals of various materials and their forming processes, I am continually confronted by students and other individuals who are unfamiliar with the fabrication and use of composites. Many seem to regard these materials as though they possess some mystical aura of indestructibility and incomprehensible "other-world" power. As one who has used these materials in several different applications and capacities for several years now, it is one of my great thrills to open up the world of composites to others and make them accessible to those who show an interest in putting these materials to the test. As has been demonstrated through several examples in this text, the fundamental processes behind the creation of a composite laminate are very straightforward and accessible to most do-it-yourselfers. Hopefully, the simple processes shown in this book have been of benefit to even the most inexperienced of fabricators, ultimately inspiring and empowering them to design, layup, and finish composites on their own.

The processes showcased in this book barely scratch the surface of what is possible with composites. As mentioned in the introduction, there are several aspects of composites design and manufacture that have not been covered, simply because there is not enough space in such a cursory text to contain every possible application and use of these unique materials. For that reason, I would encourage the reader to explore additional resources to further round out their understanding of this intriguing topic. For those interested in applying these principles for mass-manufacture (even if only for low-volume production), sources and examples from the automotive and aerospace industries can be helpful. Individuals interested in optimizing composites for competitive applications may find some interest in further readings that cover the topics of vacuum-bagging, vacuum-assisted resin transfer molding, and sandwich core construction. And even if your interest in composites is reserved for less demanding applications, studying alternative mold-making and forming techniques (such as silicone "mother" molds or even boat construction) may be beneficial to your understanding of how to use composites for a variety of applications.

Whatever your particular attraction to composites may be, seeking out other available resources will expand your understanding of these materials and greatly enhance your ability to apply them in a broad range of fabrication situations. And while a theoretical knowledge of composites is important, do not underestimate the importance of getting your hands dirty to increase your confidence in actually using them. Lastly, remember that the field of composites is still relatively new (compared to metals and woods), and there are many new methods that can still be discovered and developed—leaving many exciting possibilities for those who are willing to explore and push the envelope of their constructive imagination.

Glossary of Terms

AFRP – Abbreviation for "Aramid Fiber Reinforced Plastic"

Aluminized Fiberglass – Fiberglass that has a thin, shiny deposit of aluminum on its fibers.

Aramid – A synthetic fiber with excellent strength and abrasion resistance. DuPont manufactures such fibers under the brand name of "Kevlar".

Aromatic Polyamide – The chemical name for a synthetic fiber called an "aramid".

Autoclave – Any pressurized oven that is used as a means to produce high-quality laminate composites.

Basalt – A type of reinforcement manufactured from basalt rock.

Basket Weave – A weave of reinforcement that has two or more fiber bundles woven over and under two or more other fiber bundles.

Black Fiberglass – A type of fiberglass made to have the appearance of carbon fiber, though it does not contain the same properties as carbon.

Bladder – A specially constructed bag into which air or fluid is pressurized as a means to push a laminate against the sides of a closed mold.

Boron – A stiff and lightweight reinforcement used primarily in aerospace applications.

Buck – See "Plug"

Caliper – A measurement device with jaws and a display that can very accurately determine the thickness of a reinforcement or laminate.

Captive Mold – A mold around which a laminate is laid-up. These particular molds are not removed from the laminate once it has cured.

Carbon Fiber – A high strength and high stiffness reinforcement made from long strands of specially arranged carbon molecules.

Catalyst – A chemical that accelerates the curing of polyester and vinylester resins.

CFRP – Abbreviation for "Carbon Fiber Reinforced Plastic".

Colloidal Silica – A lightweight thickening agent that can be used for both epoxy and polyester resins.

Composite Tooling – Molds for the forming of composites that are constructed of composite materials themselves.

Composite(s) – Any material that consists of two or more other dissimilar materials. In the case of an "advanced composite", the material consists of a resin "matrix" and a fiber "reinforcement".

Compression Molding – A composites molding method that forms a composite by pressing the laminate into a form from two or more directions.

Compressive Strength – The amount of force a material can sustain when pressure is applied to it.

Consolidation Pressure – The pressure applied to a laminate, usually for the purpose of eliminating voids within the composite.

Cross-linking – The chemical bonding of molecules within a thermoset resin that solidifies the resin.

Cure – The change of a thermoset resin from liquid to solid.

Delamination – Separation between layers or plies in a laminate composite.

Demolding – Removing a composite from a mold.

Draft – The angle of a mold's walls in relation to the direction that a part will be removed from the mold.

Drape – The flexibility of a fabric.

Drapeability – A fabric's ability to lay into complexly shaped molds.

Dry Layup – The layup of any composite in which liquid resin is not actually handled by the fabricator.

Dyneema – Trade name for a particular fiber form of ultra high molecular weight polyethylene (UHMW) used in some specialty composites.

E-glass – Electrical grade fiberglass used extensively for its low cost.

Epoxy Resin – A liquid thermoset polymer used in composites that solidifies through the addition of a special hardener.

Epoxy Surface Coat – Specially formulated epoxy containing thickeners and pigment that is applied as a coating for the surface of a composite.

Exotherm – Short for "exothermic reaction".

Exothermic Reaction – A chemical reaction through which heat is released. Thermoset resins typically create such reactions.

Expanded Styrene Foam – A type of styrene foam formed by the heating and expansion of styrene beads. Typically used in protective packaging for consumer goods or as insulation in construction.

Extruded Styrene Foam – A type of styrene foam typically used as insulation for homes.

Female Mold – A mold that has a cavity in which a composite is formed to have a smooth outer face.

Fiberglass – A form of glass fiber used as a reinforcement in a wide range of advanced composites.

Filament – A very fine, individual strand of reinforcement material.

Filament Winding – A process of molding composites through which a reinforcement is taken from a spool, wetted with resin, and pulled in a continuous winding process over a form or mandrel.

Fill – Fibers that run perpendicular to the length of a woven fabric.

Fillet – A uniformly rounded edge or corner.

Finishing Resin – Polyester resin, also known as a surface coat, top coat, "waxed" resin, that forms a seal over itself to allow for complete cure of the exposed resin surface.

Flange – A flat area to a mold that extends perpendicularly from the edge of the molding surface.

Flash Tape – Special tape that can be placed in a mold and used as release for thermoset resins.

Flood Coat – A special clear resin coating applied over a composite for aesthetic purposes.

Formica – Trade name for popular counter-top laminate.

FRP – Abbreviation for "Fiber Reinforced Plastic".

Gel Coat – A thick coating of polyester resin used to protect a composite from abrasion, ultraviolet rays, and other environmental hazards.

Gel Coat Gauge – A small tool that measures the thickness of a gel coat.

GFRP – Abbreviation for "Glass Fiber Reinforced Plastic". Commonly referred to as "fiberglass".

Glass Fiber – Also referred to as "fiberglass", these reinforcements are made of high tensile strength glass fibers.

Graphite Fiber – Also referred to as "carbon fiber", these reinforcements have higher properties that typical carbon filaments.

Heat Shrink Tape – Special plastic tape that shrinks in length when heated.

Heat Shrink Tubing – Specialized flexible plastic tubing that shrinks in diameter when heated.

Hybrid Fiber – Interwoven fibers of different reinforcement types.

Impregnation – The process of infusing a reinforcement with a liquid thermoset resin.

Kevlar – Trade name for an aramid reinforcement fiber developed by DuPont.

Kevlar-29 – A grade of Kevlar used for general industrial and protective armor purposes.

Kevlar-49 – A grade of Kevlar used for high-performance and transportation applications.

Laminate – Layers of material joined together by means of chemical bonding.

Laminating Resin – Thermoset resin used specifically for laminating multiple layers of a composite into a mold.

Lamination – The build-up of several layers of composite material over a form.

Lathe – A machine used to spin a piece of material for the purpose of cutting it into a rounded shape.

Layup – A process used to infuse resin into a reinforcement and place it into a mold.

Male Mold – A mold form over which a laminate is laid to produce smooth inner surfaces.

Mandrel – A long mold of uniform cross-section used to form tubular or hollow composites.

Master – See "Plug".

Mat – A form of non-woven fabric in which short strands of fiber are held together with a binder.

Matched Mold – A two-sided closed mold used to produce a composite part that is smooth on both sides.

Matrices – The plural form of "matrix".

Matrix – In an advanced composite, the thermoset resin component of a composite.

MDF (Medium Density Fiberboard) – An engineered wood product without grain, typically used in mold-making and for other composites-related construction.

MEKP (methyl ethyl keytone peroxide) – A catalyst used with polyester and vinylester resins.

Melamine – A plastic that is produced in sheet form and laminated to boards to form durable, non-porous surfaces.

Moldless Composite – A type of composite that is constructed without the use of a mold form by laminating composite materials over foam.

Mold-release – A chemical agent that prevents resin from bonding to a mold.

Mold Core – A removable inner mold, typically used in conjunction with another mold.

Multi-part Mold – A mold that has removable mold sections for the purpose of forming complex part geometries.

Naphtha – A solvent that is very helpful in breaking down oils.

NIOSH (National Institute for Occupational Safety and Health) – A federal agency that monitors occupational safety and work environments and makes recommendations to help ensure worker safety.

Nitrile – A type of synthetic rubber that is hypo-allergenic and used in safety gloves.

Non-woven Reinforcements – Reinforcement fabrics held together by means other than typical weaving methods.

Parting Line – A line at which the parting plane intersects a part and mold surface.

Parting Plane – An imaginary plane that divides multiple mold sections.

Paste Wax – A mold release agent that is wiped onto a mold surface and then buffed to a high sheen.

Peel Strength – The resistance of a laminate to its layers being peeled apart.

Phenolic – A thermoset resin with high heat resistance properties.

Plain Weave – A weave style in which one fiber strand in the fill direction goes over and under one strand at a time in the warp direction.

Plug – A form over which composite tooling is created to make a mold.

Ply – A layer of composite material in a laminate.

Polyamide – A synthetic molecule used in the production of aramid reinforcements.

Polyester Resin – A common, inexpensive thermoset resin used extensively in boat building and for some consumer goods.

Polyethylene – A thermoplastic that is widely used for disposable and recyclable consumer goods.

Polymer – A large molecule composed of smaller hydrocarbon and other molecules and found in plastics.

Polymeric Composite – A composite composed of a plastic resin (either thermoset or thermoplastic) surrounding a fiber reinforcement.

Polypropylene – A thermoplastic used for a variety of consumer goods.

Pot Life – The amount of time a thermoset resin remains usable once catalyzed and left in its mixing container.

Pressure Vessel – A hollow composite structure used to hold pressurized gases or liquids.

Print Through – A weave pattern produced on the surface of a composite when it is heated or absorbs moisture.

PVA (Polyvinyl Alcohol) – A mold-release agent that is applied in liquid form, but dries into a very thin protective film.

Quartz - A type of reinforcement manufactured from quartz rock.

Rasp – A hand tool with sharp protrusions typically used for shaping wood.

Registration – Features in a mold that promote the alignment of multiple mold sections.

140

Reinforcements – Short or long fibers that help strengthen a plastic material.

Resin – A polymer-based chemical that exhibits plastic properties.

Resin System – The combination of a thermoset resin and a catalyst or hardener.

Rigidized Acrylic – A form of composite that uses polyester or vinylester resin and a reinforcement fiber to strengthen an acrylic plastic form.

Roll-wrapping – A process of lamination whereby a composite is wrapped around a mandrel and allowed to cure.

Roving – Thick bundles of reinforcement fiber, typically of fiberglass.

Rubbing Compound – A polishing agent that contains fine abrasive particles.

Satin Weave – A weave style that lies very flat and can be used for complex surface shapes.

Sealant Tape – A sticky silicone tape used in vacuum-bagging and other composites manufacturing procedures.

Secondary Bond – Bonding between composite materials that have already cured completely.

S-glass – A high-performance type of fiberglass used in aerospace and competition composites.

Shape Gauge – A hand tool that measures curvature of a surface for the purpose of comparing it to a template or other standard.

Shear Strength – The strength of a material to resist tearing.

Shrink Rate – The amount of shrinkage exhibited by a thermoset resin from its liquid to sold state.

Shrinkage – A reduction in volume or geometric dimension.

Sizing – Special coatings applied to filaments to make them more easily processed and used in composites.

Sleeve – Reinforcement that is helically woven (like a spring) to produce a long tube.

Sock – See "Sleeve".

Solvent – A chemical agent used to break down the molecular bonds of another chemical.

Strand – A bundle of reinforcement filaments.

Styrene Foam – A type of foam made from styrene plastic.

Styrene Monomer – A liquid chemical constituent of polyester and vinylester resins.

Surface Coat – A protective coating of resin over a composite, typically consisting of epoxy.

Tensile Modulus – A material's ability to be pulled and return to its original shape.

Tensile Strength – The strength exhibited by a material when a pulling force is applied to it.

Thermoplastic – Any polymer-based plastic that can be repeatedly heated and reformed.

Thermoset – Any polymer-based plastic that begins primarily in a liquid or gel state and irreversibly solidifies through the addition of a chemical catalyst or hardener.

Tooling Fabric – Heavy woven reinforcement fabrics typically utilized in the construction of composite tooling.

Top Coat – See "Finishing Resin".

Tow – A bundle of filaments, typically of carbon or aramid fiber, supplied in large spools.

Tubing – See "Sleeve".

Twill Weave – A weave style that is highly formable and produces interesting weave patterns.

Undercut – Any part of a mold that possesses reverse draft and may keep a part from releasing from a mold.

Unidirectional Fiber – A fabric in which the majority of the fibers are aligned in one single direction.

Urethane Foam – Hard foam composed of polyisocyanurate plastic widely used in mold making for composite tooling.

Vacuum-bagging – A composites manufacturing process that employs a flexible plastic film, sealed over an open mold, in which a vacuum is created to provide consolidation pressure from the surrounding atmosphere to push the composite against the sides of the mold.

Veil – A non-woven fabric containing short, fine diameter fibers bound together.

Veneer – A thin covering for another surface, usually from wood or plastic.

Vinyl Foam – A form of polyvinylchloride (PVC) used in composite structures and mold-making.

Vinylester Resin – A thermoset resin with good physical and chemical properties that solidifies through the addition of a catalyst.

Viscosity – A liquid's resistance to flow. High viscosity fluids are thick, while low viscosity fluids are thin.

Volatile Organic Compound (VOC) – Organic chemical compounds that have high pressure in vapor form, and are often hazardous to one's health.

Warp – Woven fibers that run the length of a fabric.

Weft – See "Fill".

Wet Layup – Any procedure for creating a composite laminate that requires the fabricator to actually handle liquid resin.

Wet-out – The ability of a reinforcement to be easily saturated with resin, or the ability of a resin to easily saturate reinforcements.

Woof – See "Fill".

Working Time – The amount of time required for a thermoset resin to solidify once it has been catalyzed or mixed with hardener, and removed from its mixing container.

Woven Reinforcement – The fiber component of a composite that has been produced using traditional textile weaving equipment.

Woven Roving – A heavy woven fabric consisting of bundles of fiber in the form of roving rather than twisted yarns.

Yarn – Bundles of fiber that are twisted to produce a flatter woven fabric.

Yield Strength – The force a material can have acting upon it before it begins to permanently deform.

Zylon – A synthetic fiber with properties similar to Kevlar.

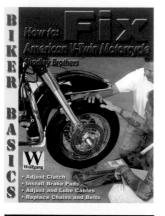

HOW TO FIX AMERICAN V-TWIN MC

Ownership of a modern American Motorcycle – no matter how good it is – requires certain mechanical skills. This new book from Wolfgang covers all the skills needed to do basic maintenance and repairs. From adjusting the clutch cable to installing brake pads, this book explains in both words and photos how to do your own work. Instead of taking the bike back to the dealer or shop where you bought it, roll it into your garage and do it yourself.

When you're trying to learn something for the first time, there's nothing like a good photo, or series of photos, that show exactly how the operation is performed.

There is no such thing as a maintenance free motorcycle. Save money and gain satisfaction. Learn how to do your own repairs in your own small shop with this new book.

Ten Chapters   144 Pages $27.95   Over 500 photos, 100% color

TATTOO - FROM IDEA TO INK

Tattoo: From Idea To Ink traces the origin of a tattoo from its initial inception through the process of design and finally implementation in the hands of talented artists like Amanda Wachob of Blue Moon Tattoo in Buffalo, New York. With an abundance of colorful images and insightful text, this book provides a first-hand look at the stages a custom client experiences in getting the tattoo of his or her dreams. From understanding this process and

reviewing the different styles of art available, Tattoo: From Idea to Ink, offers artwork, artists, and suggestions for anyone looking for that perfect piece of art. In addition to a full section filled with original artwork from master tattooists, the book features work by industry legends like Brandon Bond, Sarah Peacock, Zsolt Sarkozi, Shannon Schober, Mario Desa, Corey Rogers, Josh Woods, Nate Beavers, and many more.

Eleven Chapters   144 Pages $24.95   Over 400 photos, 100% color

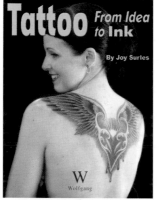

ADVANCED TATTOO ART

The art of the tattoo has emerged from the garage to the parlor, from the local bar to the boardroom. With interest in tattoos at a high point, the time is right for a detailed look at the art, and the artists, who create the elaborate designs.

Doug Mitchel take the reader inside the shops of ten well-known and very experienced artists spread across the country. Both a how-to book and a photo-intense look the world or tattoos; Tattoo Art

includes interviews with the artists that explain not only how they do what they do, but also their personal preference for materials and methods. Detailed photo sequences follow each artist through a tattoo project. From customer concept, to sketch, outline, and the finished colorful design. The chapters document not only the techniques, but also the inks and tools used during each step of the process

Ten Chapters   144 Pages $24.95   Over 400 photos, 100% color

ADVANCED PINSTRIPE ART

Since the days of Von Dutch, hot rod and motorcycle enthusiasts have used pinstripes both as stand-alone art, and as a compliment to a flame or graphic paint job.

Each chapter presents one start-to-finish project and an interview with the artist. The photo sequences take the viewer from the initial sketch to the finished design. Text explains each step of the artwork; the interviews explain the artist's choice

for paint and brushes. The artwork, often complimented with gold leaf or airbrush colors, is done on panels as well as vehicles and components. Pinstripe Art brings the reader into the shop of some of this country's best pinstripe artists, for an intense and intimate how-to lesson. This is pinstripe school, taught by masters, brought to your own home or shop.

Eleven Chapters   144 Pages $24.95   Over 400 photos, 100% color

More Great Books From Wolfgang Publications!
http://www.wolfpub.com

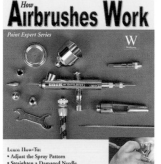

HOW AIRBRUSHES WORK

How Airbrushes Work is a comprehensive look at airbrush use, maintenance and repair. The book begins with a brief look at airbrush history, then moves to a discussion of the various airbrush types. This new book from Wolfgang Publications explains how to disassemble, clean and repair all the major brands. Even the best airbrush in the world isn't any good without a source of air. Steve discusses different compressor types and the advantages or disadvantages of each.

Two chapters explain airbrush painting basics, Steve closes the book with a gallery of airbrush art, and an airbrush buyer's guide to help readers choose wisely when they buy their first, or their fifth, airbrush.

| Ten Chapters | 144 Pages | $27.95 | Over 500 photos, 100% color |

ADVANCED AIRBRUSH ART

Like a video done with still photography, this new book is made up entirely of photo sequences that illustrate each small step in the creation of an airbrushed masterpiece. Watch as well-known masters like Vince Goodeve, Chris Cruz, Steve Wizard and Nick Pastura start with a sketch and end with a NASCAR helmet or motorcycle tank covered with graphics, murals, pinups or all of the above.

Interviews explain each artist's preference for paint and equipment, and secrets learned over decades of painting. Projects include a chrome eagle surrounded by reality flames, a series of murals, and a variety of graphic designs.

This is a great book for anyone who takes their airbrushing seriously and wants to learn more.

| Ten Chapters | 144 Pages | $24.95 | Over 400 photos, 100% color |

PRO AIRBRUSH TIPS & TECHNIQUES WITH VINCE GOODEVE

Written by well-known Airbrush artist Vince Goodeve, this book explains a lifetime's worth of learning. Follow Vince through multiple photo sequences that explain his choice of color, sense of design and preference for tools and materials. Chapters explain shop set up and preparations of the metal canvas. Ten start-to-finish sequences walk the reader through Vince's airbrush work with both motorcycles and cars. Projects include simple graphics as well as complex and intricate designs.

Accustomed to teaching, Vince uses a style that is easy to follow and understand. His enthusiasm for the airbrush comes through, making the text easy to follow. Vince has something to say to all airbrush artists – whether beginner or advanced.

| Fifteen Chapters | 144 Pages | $24.95 | Over 500 photos, 100% color |

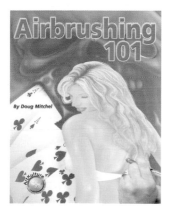

AIR BRUSHING 101

Airbrushing 101 presents a series of start-to-finish projects, each painted by a different artist, and each designed to illustrate a different type of airbrushing. Author Doug Mitchel and the artists in the book introduce a wide range of airbrushing categories, including: fire art/illustration, T-shirts, automotive, fingernails, body and face painting, hip hop and model painting.

All the start-to-finish photo sequences are designed for first-time airbrush users. In addition to the sequences, well illustrates the basic strokes that form the foundation for nearly all airbrush art. Doug Mitchel uses interviews to explore the way in which each artist learned his or her skills, what type of paint they prefer, how they adjust their airbrush, and how to avoid the typical beginner's mistakes.

| Ten Chapters | 144 Pages | $27.95 | Over 400 photos, 100% color |

Additional Readings & Resources

Reference Chapter 1

McBeath, Simon. Competition Car Composites. Sparkford, UK: Haynes Publishing, 2000

Aird, Forbes. Fiberglass & Other Composite Materials. New York, NY: HP Books, 2006

Birch, Stuart "Lotus Small and Maneuverable." Automotive Engineering International, 116, no. 6 (May 2008).

Sourcebook 2008 – The International Guide to Products & Services for the Composites Industry. Vol. 16-A, Gardner Publications (January 2008)

High Performance Composites magazine

Composites Technology magazine

Composites World magazine

Composites Manufacturing magazine

Reference Chapter 2

www.azom.com
www.matweb.com
www.hexcel.com
www2.dupont.com
www.sollercomposites.com
www.compositesone.com
www.acma.net
www.westsystem.com

Marshall, Andrew C., Composite Basics, 7th ed. Walnut Creek, CA : Marshall Consulting, 2005

Wiley, Jack. The Fiberglass Repair and Construction Handbook, 2nd ed. Summit, PA: Tab Books, 1988.

Reference Chapter 3

Additional Readings and Resources

Gougeon Brothers, Inc. West System User Manual & Product Guide. 2008.

System Three Resins, Inc. The Epoxy Book. 2004.

Reference Chapter 4

www.shopscissors.com
A good resource for scissors of all kinds.

www.sollercomposites.com
Reasonably priced retailer of sock/sleeve composites and fabrics along with specialty heat shrink tubing materials.

www.fibreglast.com
Supplier of several specialty composites fabrication tools and materials for basic and advanced composites.

www.msc.com or www.grainger.com
Large retailers of industrial equipment and supplies.

Reference Chapter 6

www.sollercomposites.com

www.rqriley.com/frp-foam.htm

http://hotwirefoamfactory.com/home.php

http://www.techlib.com/hobby/hotwire_foam_cutter.htm